ROSA
PARKS

The
Movement
Organizes

The History of the
Civil Rights Movement

ELLA BAKER: A Leader Behind the Scenes

STOKELY CARMICHAEL: The Story of Black Power

FANNIE LOU HAMER: From Sharecropping to Politics

JESSE JACKSON: Still Fighting for the Dream

MARTIN LUTHER KING, JR.: The Dream of Peaceful Revolution

MALCOLM X: Another Side of the Movement

THURGOOD MARSHALL: The Fight for Equal Justice

ROSA PARKS: The Movement Organizes

A. PHILIP RANDOLPH: Integration in the Workplace

ROSA PARKS

The Movement Organizes

by Kai Friese

With an Introduction by
ANDREW YOUNG

Silver Burdett Press

Series Consultant: Aldon Morris

Cover and Text Design: Design Five, New York
Maps: General Cartography, Inc.
Series Editorial Supervisor: Richard G. Gallin
Series Supervision of Art and Design: Leslie Bauman
Series Editing: Agincourt Press
Developmental Editor: Della Rowland

Consultants: Dr. Elysa Robinson, COMPACT Coordinator, Detroit Public
Schools, Detroit, Michigan; Catherine J. Lenix-Hooker, Deputy Chief, Schomburg
Center for Research in Black Culture, New York Public Library.

Permissions and photo credits appear on page 128.

Library of Congress Cataloging-in-Publication Data

Friese, Kai.
   Rosa Parks: the movement organizes / by Kai Jabir Friese; with an introduction
by Andrew Young.
     p.   cm. —(The History of the civil rights movement)
   Contents: Includes bibliographical references and index.
   Summary: A biography of the Alabama black woman whose refusal to give up
her seat on a bus helped establish the civil rights movement.
   1. Parks, Rosa, 1913–   —Juvenile literature. 2. Afro-Americans—Alabama—
Montgomery—Biography—Juvenile literature. 3. Civil rights workers—Alabama—
Montgomery—Biography—Juvenile literature. 4. Montgomery (Ala.)—
Biography—Juvenile literature. 5. Afro-Americans—Civil rights—Alabama—
Montgomery—Juvenile literature. 6. Montgomery (Ala.)—Race relations—Juvenile
Literature. 7. Segregation in transportation—Alabama—Montgomery—History—
20th century—Juvenile literature. [1. Parks, Rosa, 1913- . 2. Afro-Americans—
Biography. 3. Afro-Americans—Civil Rights.]
   I. Title
F334.M753P384   1990
323'.092—dc20
[B]
[92]   90-32009
ISBN 0-382-09927-3 (lib bdg.)   CIP
ISBN 0-382-24065-0 (pbk.)   AC

CONTENTS

Introduction by Andrew Young vi

Civil Rights Movement Time Line 2

Chapter 1 **The Convention** 5

     2 **A Southern Childhood** 8

     3 **The Cradle of the Confederacy** 18

     4 **Living with Jim Crow** 26

     5 **Students of Protest** 36

     6 **The Highlander School** 45

     7 **Don't Ride the Bus on Monday** 52

     8 **Monday Morning** 61

     9 **The Walking City** 68

    10 **Paying the Price** 76

    11 **The Supreme Court Decides** 81

    12 **The Segregationists Fight Back** 86

    13 **The Civil Rights Movement** 92

    14 **Voting Rights** 104

    15 **The Mother of the Movement** 110

Timetable of Events in the Life of Rosa Parks 122

Suggested Reading 123

Sources 124

Index 125

INTRODUCTION

By Andrew Young

Some thirty years ago, a peaceful revolution took place in the United States, as African Americans sought equal rights. That revolution, which occurred between 1954 and 1968, is called the civil rights movement. Actually, African Americans have been struggling for their civil rights for as long as they have been in this country. Before the Civil War, brave abolitionists were calling out for an end to the injustice and cruelty of slavery. Even after the Civil War freed slaves, African Americans were still forced to fight other forms of racism and discrimination—segregation and prejudice. This movement still continues today as people of color battle racial hatred and economic exploitation all over the world.

The books in this series tell the stories of the lives of Ella Baker, Stokely Carmichael, Fannie Lou Hamer, Jesse Jackson, Malcolm X, Thurgood Marshall, Rosa Parks, A. Philip Randolph, and Martin Luther King, Jr.—just a few of the thousands of brave people who worked in the civil rights movement. Learning about these heroes is an important lesson in American history. They risked their homes and their jobs—and some gave their lives—to secure rights and freedoms that we now enjoy and often take for granted.

Most of us know the name of Dr. Martin Luther King, Jr., the nonviolent leader of the movement. But others who were just as important may not be as familiar. Rosa Parks insisted on her right to a seat on a public bus. Her action started a bus boycott that changed a segregation law and sparked a movement.

Ella Baker was instrumental in founding two major civil rights organizations, the Southern Christian Leadership Conference (SCLC) and the Student Nonviolent Coordinating Committee (SNCC). One of the chairpersons of SNCC, Stokely Carmichael, is perhaps best known for making the slogan "Black Power" famous. Malcolm X, the strong voice from the urban north, rose from a prison inmate to a powerful black Muslim leader.

Not many people know that the main organizer of the 1963 March on Washington was A. Philip Randolph. Younger leaders called Randolph the "father of the movement." Fannie Lou Hamer, a poor sharecropper from Mississippi, was such a powerful speaker for voters rights that President Lyndon Johnson blocked out television coverage of the 1964 Democratic National Convention to keep her off the air. Thurgood Marshall was the first African American to be made a Supreme Court justice.

Many who demanded equality paid for their actions. They were fired from their jobs, thrown out of their homes, beaten, and even killed. But they marched, went to jail, and put their lives on the line over and over again for the right to equal justice. These rights include something as simple as being able to sit and eat at a lunch counter. They include political rights such as the right to vote. They also include the equal rights to education and job opportunities that lead to economic betterment.

We are now approaching a level of democracy that allows all citizens of the United States to participate in the American dream. Jesse Jackson, for example, has pursued the dream of the highest office in this land, the president of the United States. Jackson's running for president was made possible by those who went before him. They are the people whose stories are included in this biography and history series, as well as thousands of others who remain nameless. They are people who depend upon you to carry on the dream of liberty and justice for all people of the world.

Civil Rights Movement Time Line

—1954——1955——1956——1957—

May 17—
Brown v. *Board of Education of Topeka I:* Supreme Court rules racial segregation in public is unconstitutional.

May 31—
Brown v. *Board of Education of Topeka II:* Supreme Court says desegregation of public schools must proceed "with all deliberate speed."

August 28—
14-year-old Emmett Till is killed in Money, Mississippi.

December 5, 1955–December 20, 1956—
Montgomery, Alabama bus boycott.

November 13—
Supreme Court outlaws racial segregation on Alabama's city buses.

January 10, 11—
Southern Christian Leadership Conference (SCLC) is founded.

August 29—
Civil Rights Act is passed. Among other things, it creates Civil Rights Commission to advise the president and gives government power to uphold voting rights.

September 1957–
Little Rock Central High School is desegregated.

—1962——1963——1964—

September 29—
Federal troops help integrate University of Mississippi ("Ole Miss") after two people are killed and several are injured.

April to May—
Birmingham, Alabama, demonstrations. School children join the marches.

May 20—
Supreme Court rules Birmingham's segregation laws are unconstitutional.

June 12—
NAACP worker Medgar Evers is killed in Jackson, Mississippi.

August 28—
March on Washington draws more than 250,000 people.

September 15—
Four girls are killed when a Birmingham church is bombed.

November 22—
President John F. Kennedy is killed in Dallas, Texas.

March–June—
St. Augustine, Florida, demonstrations.

June 21—
James Chaney, Michael Schwerner, and Andrew Goodman are killed while registering black voters in Mississippi.

July 2—
Civil Rights Act is passed. Among other things, it provides for equal job opportunities and gives the government power to sue to desegregate public schools and facilities.

August—
Mississippi Freedom Democratic Party (MFDP) attempts to represent Mississippi at the Democratic National Convention.

1958 — 1959 — 1960 — 1961

September 1958–August 1959—
Little Rock Central High School is closed because governor refuses to integrate it.

February 1—
Student sit-ins at lunch counter in Greensboro, North Carolina, begin sit-in protests all over the South.

April 17—
Student Nonviolent Coordinating Committee (SNCC) is founded.

May 6—
Civil Rights Act is passed. Among other things, it allows judges to appoint people to help blacks register to vote.

Eleven African countries win their independence.

May 4—
Freedom Rides leave Washington, D.C., and head south.

September 22—
Interstate Commerce Commission ordered to enforce desegregation laws on buses, and trains, and in travel facilities like waiting rooms, rest rooms, and restaurants.

1965 — 1966 — 1967 — 1968

January–March—
Selma, Alabama, demonstrations.

February 21—
Malcolm X is killed in New York City.

March 21–25—
More than 25,000 march from Selma to Montgomery, Alabama.

August 6—
Voting Rights Act passed.

August 11–16—
Watts riot (Los Angeles, California).

June—
James Meredith "March Against Fear" from Memphis, Tennessee, to Jackson, Mississippi. Stokely Carmichael makes slogan "Black Power" famous during march.

Fall—
Black Panther Party for Self-Defense is formed by Huey Newton and Bobby Seale in Oakland, California.

June 13—
Thurgood Marshall is appointed first African-American U.S. Supreme Court justice.

Summer—
Riots break out in 30 U.S. cities.

April 4—
Martin Luther King, Jr., is killed in Memphis, Tennessee.

April 11—
Civil Rights Act is passed. Among other things, it prohibits discrimination in selling and renting houses or apartments.

May 13–June 23—
Poor People's March: Washington, D.C., to protest poverty.

1 THE CONVENTION

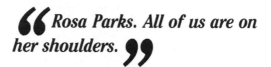

66 *Rosa Parks. All of us are on her shoulders.* 99

JESSE JACKSON, at the 1988 Democratic National Convention

O n Monday, July 18, 1988, the meeting room of the Marriott Marquis Hotel in Atlanta, Georgia, was packed with 1,200 people. They were waiting to hear whether Jesse Jackson would be running beside Michael Dukakis as a candidate for vice president. For months Jackson had run an incredible campaign as a presidential candidate. He had been Dukakis's opponent for the Democratic party's nomination. This was the closest any African American had ever come to becoming president of the United States. Now he would have to go into that room and tell his delegates, the people who had

Rosa Parks and Jesse Jackson at the 1988 Democratic National Convention, as they appeared on television.

spent months supporting the campaign, that his run for the White House was over. But he also wanted them to realize that it wasn't all over—there would be more elections and more campaigns in the years to come. When they saw the woman beside him, perhaps they would understand that they shouldn't lose hope just because they had a long road ahead.

The room was filled with shouts and cries as Jackson walked in. But the delegates were instantly hushed by his opening words: "Rosa Parks. All of us are on her shoulders." He paused to let his words sink in along with the sight of the silver-haired woman beside him. Although many people in the room had never seen her before, they had read the name and seen pictures of this quiet, dignified woman many times. They understood Jackson's words immediately. This was the woman who had swept the headlines of newspapers by a simple act of courage more than 30 years ago. With one act of defiance, she had begun a huge protest movement that changed the lives of millions of Americans.

It was in the 1950s that Mrs. Parks's name became known all around the country. In those days, black people were often prevented from voting in an election. At that time, only a white man could dream of becoming the president of the United States. It was only after a long struggle in which thousands of people took part that black people gained the rights that white citizens had always enjoyed. Today that struggle is remembered as the civil rights movement.

This book tells the story of a little girl named Rosa Mc-Cauley, who grew up to be Rosa Parks—the "mother of the movement."

A SOUTHERN CHILDHOOD

***"Children have their sorrows as well as men and women...."*

FREDERICK DOUGLASS
abolitionist leader

Some 70 years before the Democratic National Convention in Atlanta, a little girl name Rosa Louise McCauley lay in bed wide-eyed with fear. It was well past her bedtime, as her mother kept telling her, but she wouldn't feel safe until she saw the sun come up on her family in the morning. The Klan was riding—the Ku Klux Klan—and there was no telling whom they would attack tonight. Rosa's grandfather, Sylvester Edwards, had his gun out as usual. But it didn't make much difference. She was old enough to know that an old man with an ancient shotgun didn't have much of a chance against a pack of vicious Klansmen armed with the best six-guns and Winchester rifles money could buy.

For Rosa and many other children in the town of Pine Level (near Tuskegee), Alabama, the Klan members were far more terrifying than any boogeyman or monster they could imagine. The Klansmen, or Kluxers, as people called them, often dressed up in strange hooded uniforms that looked like Halloween ghost costumes. Rosa knew that there were grown men underneath those hoods. Some of them might even be neighbors. Many of them were ordinary family men, farmers, and businessmen. But all of them were white men, and for blacks these Klansmen spelled danger. Members of the Ku Klux Klan believed that whites were superior to, or better than, blacks. They thought it was their duty to terrorize the black population.

All across the southern states there were chapters of "white knights," as the Klansmen liked to call themselves. They would ride out regularly displaying their weapons and firing them wildly as they went past the homes of black people. Sometimes they would stop and leave a burning cross in front of someone's house as a warning. Many times these warnings were followed by murder. The Klan was particularly fond of lynchings. They would kidnap a black man, beat and torture him, then hang him from a tree and leave him there to die. The Klan's victims were often men who had refused to be pushed around. But they might just as easily be people who had the bad luck to stumble upon a group of Klansmen in an ugly mood.

Rosa McCauley had heard enough grim tales about the Klan to keep her from sleeping a wink that night. When morning came, she breathed a sigh of relief. The ordeal was over. Her grandparents, her mother, Leona, and her little brother Sylvester were all safe. But there was no knowing when the brutal white men would ride again.

Ever since World War I had ended in 1918, it seemed as if they were always riding. People said it was because they were scared of the young black veterans who were coming back from the

The Ku Klux Klan burns a cross as part of its violence and terror against African Americans.

trenches in France. The soldiers had fought in muddy battlefields for years. Sitting in the damp trenches they dug to protect themselves from the enemy, they lived through artillery and poison-gas attacks. They had fought beside men from all over the world—black men like themselves from North Africa, brown-skinned men from India, as well as many European whites. Together they had stormed the trenches of their German enemy and won the war. The returning soldiers had many tales of how different life was outside the United States. In Europe, they said, blacks were treated almost the same as whites, and they had been treated as heroes. Now, back in Alabama, many of Tuskegee's white people were afraid that these young men would be full of new ideas and full of fight. The Klan was riding to make sure the African Americans knew that nothing was going to change. They had burned churches and gone into people's homes and beaten them senseless. Rosa heard that they had even lynched a man just to make an example of him.

Grandfather Sylvester was always figuring that if the Klan came into the house, he would use his shotgun to protect the family. He actually looked forward to the day they stopped at his home. When that happened, he planned to use his shotgun to kill as many Klansmen as he could.

Rosa was proud of her grandfather, but she hoped he would never have to face the Ku Klux Klan. She knew that he wouldn't give in to them quietly. He was a brave man. He had been a slave, and he held his freedom dear. Sylvester Edwards would tell Rosa the history of her people—how they had been taken from Africa and were forced to become slaves. They had been treated cruelly for centuries. Grandfather Sylvester himself had been so brutally beaten on the plantation where he worked as a boy that he still walked with a limp.

Over the years, many words have been used in the United States to describe blacks, or African Americans. These words include *people of color* and *colored, Negro,* as well as *black* and *African American.* Depending on how a word was used, it could be insulting or reflect pride. As long as the Klan remained strong, blacks in the South would have to fight long and hard for words of pride.

Rosa heard about the many daring African Americans who had fought to free themselves and other slaves. There was the tale of Nat Turner, who had organized a slave rebellion in Virginia. Within only two days, Turner and his men showed the whites of Southampton County, Virginia, the depth of hatred black slaves felt for their masters. Within those 48 hours, Turner raised an army of 60 men. They took the lives of 57 white men, women, and children before they were defeated.

With his small army destroyed, Turner still managed to hide out in the forests, fields, and wheat stacks of the county for nearly two months while a force of 500 men searched the countryside for him. When he was finally captured, Turner freely admitted to leading the rebellion and killing white families. But when he was brought to trial, he wouldn't agree that he was guilty of any crimes.

One day in November 1831, Nat Turner was executed in front of a crowd of onlookers. He remained proud and fearless to the end, and the story of his bravery and rebelliousness became a legend for blacks.

Not all the stories Rosa heard about her people's struggles ended like Nat Turner's. There were happier tales, like that of Harriet Tubman, a former slave from Maryland who escaped to the North in 1849. Instead of simply enjoying her own freedom, Tubman began to work for the Underground Railroad. This was a group of people—both white and black—who helped hundreds of slaves escape to freedom in the northern states. Tubman and her friends would shelter and hide runaway slaves, then guide them across the Mason-Dixon Line. This line separated the South, where millions of African Americans were enslaved, from the North, where slavery was illegal. In 1850, only a year after Tubman's own escape, the new Fugitive Slave Law made it legal for slave owners to recapture runaway slaves in northern states and take them back to the South. But Harriet Tubman and the Underground Railroad wouldn't be stopped so easily. They began to take the runaway slaves farther north across the border to Canada, where they would be protected by British laws.

During the 1850s, Tubman risked her life by traveling back to the southern states to lead small groups of African Americans to freedom. Professional slave catchers followed them. Plantation owners hated Harriet Tubman so much that they offered a $40,000 reward to anyone who could capture her. But she outsmarted them all. No one was ever caught when she led an escape.

During the Civil War, when the southern states were at war

with the forces of the Union government in Washington, D.C., Harriet Tubman risked her life by going into Confederate country. By following the southern army and mixing with its troops, who took her for a harmless slave, Tubman was able to get information that would help the federal troops. But Harriet Tubman wasn't the only black person who helped to defeat the supporters of slavery. During the Civil War, thousands of young black men gave their lives fighting for the Union. Many more helped to guide the federal troops through the southern countryside. All of them must have felt the joy of victory when the Confederates surrendered in 1865. Rosa's grandfather remembered well the thrill with which he looked forward to the days of freedom. He told her how the promise of those times was lost as the freed slaves were prevented from keeping anything but the smallest patch of land on their former owners' property.

This system, called sharecropping, wasn't very different from slavery. These former slaves had no money or possessions of their own with which to start a new life. Because they couldn't pay for the land they farmed, the workers, or sharecroppers, shared their crops with their former masters. As a result, the plantation owners still had blacks working in the fields, but now they didn't have to feed or clothe them. The sharecroppers were trapped because they couldn't scrape together enough money to leave.

Many of the whites in Alabama liked to believe another version of the history of slavery. According to them, the time of slavery was a golden age in which blacks knew their place—picking cotton at the feet of their kindly white masters. The South was betrayed by the treacherous President Abraham Lincoln, they said. During the Civil War, his Yankee army had invaded the southern states, destroyed the cotton plantations, and filled the blacks' heads with foolish ideas of freedom and citizenship. Many white Alabamians looked back with pride to the war they had fought against the Yankees. They still spoke of their state capital, Montgomery, as "the cradle of the Confederacy." The Confederate alliance of southern states had been formed in Montgomery to fight the Union.

Soon after the Confederate army was defeated in 1865, white men in Alabama and other southern states began forming chapters of the Ku Klux Klan. They were worried that African Americans would become powerful now that they had been freed from slavery. It is true that during the first years after the war, many black men were given important government positions in the South by the ruling Republican party. The 15th Amendment to the U.S. Constitution gave black men the right to vote in 1870. At the same time, many southern whites were temporarily prevented from voting or standing for election because they had supported the Confederacy.

This situation made whites angry. Thousands of white men joined the Klan and other groups of night riders who terrorized blacks. Soon most southern blacks had learned that they would have to stay away from politics if they wanted to stay alive. By the late 19th century, no more African-American congressmen were being elected from the South. Blacks no longer dared to vote. In Alabama, where there had once been 140,000 black voters, only 3,472 were still registered by 1883.

Once it had driven blacks from politics, the Klan was quiet for a time. But during the last decade of the 19th century, a new wave of white violence against African Americans began. Hundreds of blacks were beaten or lynched for failing to show the respect that whites demanded of them. Many whites clung to the racist notions that they were superior to African Americans. The problem was that blacks didn't believe they were inferior to whites.

In 1915, thousands of people across the country flocked to see one of the first movies made in Hollywood. It was called *The Birth of a Nation*. The film was a great success all over the United States. It made more money than any movie had ever made before. White audiences in the South were proud to find that the film's heroes were the Klansmen. It seemed that the entire country admired them. Then, in 1917, the United States entered World War I and the army began training black men to fight in Europe. Some people in the South felt uneasy. If these men could be asked to fight for their country beside white soldiers, maybe they would demand to be equal in other ways. They didn't want any black war heroes. The Klan began to ride again, to scare any human dignity out of the local blacks.

But Rosa McCauley's family taught her to have pride in herself, her family, and her people. When she learned that some of her ancestors had been Native Americans, she was proud of that, too. She was living proof that people of different races could love one another even if it was against the law. Southern lawmakers had long ago made interracial marriages a crime. They called these marriages between people of different races miscegenation and said they were shameful and unnatural.

Rosa McCauley wasn't ashamed of her history. She knew that her birthday, February 4, 1913, was a year before World War I began in Europe and a month before Harriet Tubman died. Rosa's mother, Leona, had been working as a schoolteacher in Tuskegee, Alabama, and her father, James McCauley, was a carpenter. They had some farmland of their own. Tuskegee was known to people all over the country as the home of the great black leader Booker T. Washington and Tuskegee Institute, which he had founded. At the institute, blacks could receive training in many crafts and trades that had once been closed to them. Because of this, Rosa could take pride in her birthplace, too.

But the family didn't stay in Tuskegee long. After her little brother Sylvester was born, Rosa's father left them and went off to live in another town. He had been cheated out of his farmland by a white man and couldn't support the family any longer.

That was when Rosa and her mother and brother moved to her grandparents' farm in Pine Level, which lay between Tuskegee and Montgomery. It was just a small plot of land, but

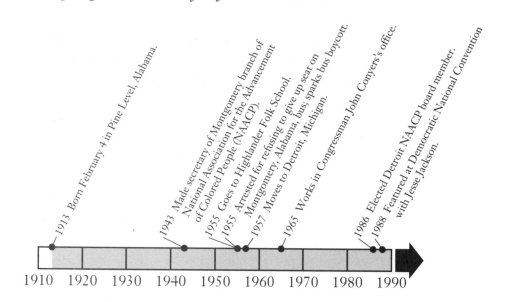

it kept them all fed. Their corn rose high above the ground, and beneath the rich black earth their peanuts and sweet potatoes grew well. Rosa often worked by her grandfather's side in the fields. As she worked, she sometimes sang a song that she had learned from her mother: "Oh freedom, oh freedom. Before I'll be a slave I'll be buried in my grave."

Rosa's mother still worked as a teacher in an African-American school. Rosa knew this wasn't the safest profession for a woman in Alabama. Her grandparents often remembered the fall of 1870, when nearly every black church and schoolhouse in Tuskegee was burned by white men. Schoolteachers—both male and female—had been attacked, and some of them had been killed.

But Mrs. McCauley wasn't afraid of the Klan. She was always telling her daughter how important it was to get an education. Blacks had struggled very hard to establish schools of their own, and they had to fight to keep them going. Rosa began to understand why so many whites hated what they called the "colored schools." In the old days, slaves were often threatened with death if they tried to learn to read and write. White people felt superior to black people because they were educated. Yet deep down, they must have realized that with the same opportunities, black children would be just as well educated as their own children were.

As it was, the schools for black children couldn't offer the same opportunities white students enjoyed. These schools had very little money to pay for trained teachers, books, or proper classrooms. Like all black children in Pine Level, Rosa went to school for only six months each year. Then the school closed down and the children went to work in the fields. White children went to school for nine months of the year. Leona McCauley's classes were held in a rickety building that was also used as a church. Her pupils always made sure they didn't leave any of their books and belongings in the schoolhouse. They were afraid the Klan would burn the building overnight. But Leona McCauley was determined to see that her daughter got the best education possible. She decided that one day when she had saved enough money, Rosa would go to school in Montgomery.

3 THE CRADLE OF THE CONFEDERACY

> **66** *There were white and colored elevators. I tried to use them as little as possible. There were white and colored water fountains, so you just didn't drink.* **99**

ROSA PARKS, remembering Montgomery

In 1924, when Rosa was 11 years old, she finished studying at the country school in Pine Level. Leona McCauley had been saving money for her daughter's education for many years now, and the time had finally come to put those savings to use. She sent Rosa to a private school for black girls in Montgomery. The school was called the Montgomery Industrial School for Girls, but most people knew it as Mrs. White's School for Girls.

Rosa's school in Pine Level had only one room and one teacher. Mrs. White's school had many classrooms and several well-trained teachers. They taught the same subjects that white children at Montgomery's white public junior-high schools were studying. But the girls at Mrs. White's also learned skills that would help them to make a living when they left school. Rosa learned to type and to stitch and sew clothes.

Rosa liked her new school, and she also liked being in Montgomery. In the past, she had come into town from time to time with her mother, but it was exciting to think that she would be here every day of the week. Downtown Montgomery, with its broad avenues and grand buildings, made quite a change from the wooden shacks and muddy paths at the edge of town where she lived. From many of those broad avenues Rosa could see the enormous white state capitol building, which seemed to dominate the city. It was here that Jefferson Davis, the president of the Confederacy, was sworn in at the start of the Civil War. Now the government of Alabama met here to create state laws—the rules and regulations that reached into the lives of every citizen.

Just across the street from the front of the capitol was another grand building that made many of Montgomery's blacks proud—the Dexter Avenue Baptist Church. With its solid brickwork, carved pews, its beautiful organ and fine location, Dexter Baptist was admired by many people. The church was started in 1877 by a congregation made up of most of the town's wealthy blacks. Now, nearly 50 years later, it remained the place of worship for the black upper class of Montgomery.

In Pine Level, where Rosa lived, it was hard to find a rich black person. Most of the people there lived a simple life on their tiny plots of land. But in Montgomery, Rosa knew, there were several well-to-do blacks who had never raised a crop in their lives. There were doctors and businessmen. There were blacks who ran stores, funeral homes, and taxi companies. There were also a number of black college professors and schoolteachers who earned a great deal more than Rosa's mother ever could in her one-room church school.

The wealthy professional blacks who were members of the Dexter Avenue Baptist Church were like a private club. They would turn out on Sundays in their finest clothes to listen to some of the best-known preachers in the country. People said that the Dexter Baptist congregation allowed only 700 members in order to keep up its private-club image.

But no matter how well the members of this "club" thought of themselves, their everyday lives were governed by laws that grouped them with the poorest blacks and beneath every white in Montgomery. These laws were called the Jim Crow laws. They forced Rosa McCauley to study in a rundown school for many years. They also prevented her from attending the well-built new public school where the local white children studied. Jim Crow laws prevented even the wealthiest blacks in Montgomery from getting a meal at most lunch counters in the city. Because of these laws, blacks on long car trips couldn't stay in a motel if they stopped for the night—unless they could find a "Colored Only" motel. Blacks riding the streetcars home from work often had to stand even when there were plenty of seats available.

Since Rosa came into Montgomery more often now, she always had to remember what she could and couldn't do because of the Jim Crow, or segregation, laws. If she wanted a drink from a public water fountain, she had to make sure it wasn't marked Whites Only. If she needed to use a public rest room, it was the same. Sometimes, when her mother gave her a little pocket money to spend, she would go to buy herself a soda. But she would then be told that the soda jerk didn't serve "niggers." Whenever Rosa caught a streetcar to or from school, she had to look to see whether there were any seats free in the tiny black section.

Rosa learned that black people in Montgomery had fought to get even those few seats provided for their use. In the year 1900, 13 years before she was born, Montgomery's blacks had boycotted, or refused to use, the streetcars because only two seats were

Sojourner Truth forced the Washington, D.C., Streetcar Company to integrate its cars.

reserved for them. The boycott had lasted only a week, but it forced the streetcar company to give more seats to the blacks.

There were similar, encouraging stories to be heard from other parts of the country. There were the famous tales of Sojourner Truth, the courageous woman who had put an end to segregated streetcars in Washington, D.C., by fighting their conductors in and out of court. Like Harriet Tubman, Sojourner Truth had been born a slave but was freed by the New York State Emancipation Act in 1827. She became well known in the North as she traveled around making speeches against slavery and in support of women's rights.

During the Civil War, Truth worked in a military hospital in Washington, D.C., caring for sick and wounded soldiers. She rode a streetcar to work every day and found that she could never get a seat in the Jim Crow car, where blacks were supposed to sit. As a black person she wasn't allowed to look for a seat in the white car, yet white people were free to take seats in the black car.

Angered by this situation, Truth wrote a letter complaining to the president of the streetcar company. As a result, the company decided to put an end to segregation on its lines. It opened all the cars to everyone. But Truth was still bothered by conductors and white passengers who didn't like the idea of sitting next to blacks. She would answer such people sharply, telling them that she knew the law. They should pay for a private carriage if they were so particular, she told them.

When one conductor made the mistake of hurting her by handling her roughly, Truth had him arrested and dismissed from his job. People soon came to accept racially integrated streetcars in Washington, D.C., and Truth noted with satisfaction that "the inside of the cars look like pepper and salt."

Sojourner Truth wasn't the only woman who fought against segregated public transportation. Mary Ellen Pleasant had fought the same battle in California. She, too, was black and an antislavery campaigner. She was also a millionaire, and she took the San Francisco Trolley Company to court in 1866 when she was told she couldn't ride one of its cars.

The stories of these brave women inspired Rosa McCauley. When she was in Montgomery, she often walked rather than use the segregated cars. If the trolley company wasn't going to treat her like a decent human being, she decided, it wasn't going to profit from her fare.

Yet it looked as if segregation would never end in Alabama. It was one thing to fight Jim Crow in Washington and California, but segregation was a treasured way of life for most white people in the South. It was a reminder of the days when some of them had been slave masters. Sometimes it even seemed that the authorities were on the lookout for more and more ways of segregating people. Rosa remembered seeing an elevator for the first time in Montgomery. Even it was segregated. When buses began to replace Montgomery's streetcars, they were segregated, too.

The white men who governed Alabama liked to say that segregation wasn't unfair. The races would stay separate, they said, but this didn't mean they were unequal. After all, it was argued, if whites wanted to stay apart from blacks, surely they had a right to do so. What was more, the law agreed with them.

They were right about the law. In 1896, the Supreme Court of the United States made a decision in the case of *Plessy* v. *Ferguson*. The justices had to decide whether or not a law that had been passed to segregate railway cars in Louisiana was in agreement with the U.S. Constitution. The Court's decision in this famous case became known as the "separate but equal" ruling. In it, the justices argued that since the Constitution already accepted blacks and whites as equal citizens, segregation did no harm. It simply allowed the two races to develop separately. To outlaw segregation, they said, would be to force the races to mix, and that shouldn't happen. "If the two races are to meet," the justices said, "it must be as a result of the voluntary consent of individuals."

Although it sounded as though the Supreme Court was protecting everyone's freedom, the "separate but equal" ruling actually forced black people to accept unfair treatment. The Court's decision allowed white lawmakers to go on creating segregation laws that affected every part of daily life in the South. For example, it was illegal for a black person and a white person to share a taxi in Montgomery, or even to play checkers together on public property. It was insulting for black people in Montgomery to be constantly treated as if they were somehow offensive to white people.

What bothered Rosa McCauley most of all wasn't the fact that she couldn't share the company of whites. The real problem was that there was no way for blacks to get equal treatment under

In most places, segregation meant water fountains and other services were separate and unequal.

segregation, no matter what the U.S. Constitution said. The "separate but equal" water fountains gave sparkling new water coolers to whites and a trickle of warm water to black people. The "separate but equal" public rest rooms for blacks were either broken most of the time or they didn't exist at all. It was the same with the schools.

By the time she was 13, Rosa had finished studying at Mrs. White's school. She had gone on to Booker T. Washington Junior High, which was a public school for black children in Montgomery. Rosa knew that the public schools for white children kept buying new equipment and buildings, while she and her classmates went to school in crumbling buildings that were never repaired.

What was equal about all this? The Supreme Court justices

couldn't have been more wrong when they said that the Constitution protected the equality of all American citizens. As long as segregation existed, white people would make sure that black people in the South were only second-class citizens.

Rosa McCauley had been learning that lesson all her life. Now, at the age of 15, as the time came for her to graduate from Booker T. Washington Junior High, the lesson was being repeated. In 1928, Montgomery still had no public high school that was open to blacks. The only choice for a student like Rosa, who was determined to finish her education, was to take high-school courses at Alabama State College. It was an unusual way to finish high school, and it would be costly, but Rosa's family insisted that they would find the money somehow. They were as good as their word, and through hard work and thriftiness they raised enough money for Rosa to begin her classes.

Rosa knew how hard it was for her family to pay her school fees, and sometimes she wanted to leave the college to help out on the farm. Grandfather Sylvester had died a few years earlier, and her grandmother, mother, and brother Sylvester were having a difficult time raising enough food and money. Then, when Rosa had only a few more courses to take in order to graduate, her grandmother, Rose, fell ill. Rosa decided to leave her studies for a while so that she could care for the old woman.

Grandmother Rose never recovered. Only months after Rosa left Alabama State, Rose Edwards died. Rosa was just about to go back to school when her mother fell ill. They had to give up the farm, and Rosa stayed home to look after her mother while Sylvester worked as a carpenter. Rosa and her mother were both sad that she hadn't finished high school. It had always been the family's dream to give Rosa a good education. Still, they had always known that the dream might not come true. The odds were against them. It was hard to think of another black family in Pine Level that had put a child through high school.

Then, in the spring of 1931, Rosa found a new reason to be happy about her life. His name was Raymond Parks.

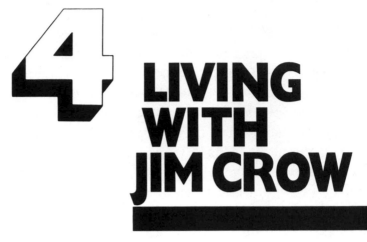

4 LIVING WITH JIM CROW

There has been a universal discrimination here in Alabama, and, indeed, all over the South, in the treatment of the colored people as to cars they are permitted to ride in.

An African-American attorney testifying against segregated travel in 1883

Raymond Parks was a man who had been deeply affected by the racial divisions in Alabama. Raymond's father was white, while his mother, Geri, was black. But Raymond's parents had never married, and he and his sister were never accepted by their father. It was almost unheard of for white men to take responsibility for their children in a situation like this. They didn't want to admit to what was then the crime of miscegenation. Instead, Raymond grew up to hate the part of him that was white. He had his father's blond hair, pale skin, and blue eyes, but white people would never accept him as one of their own. In fact, white people seemed to have a special feeling of dislike for "fair-skinned Negroes" like Raymond. Perhaps it was because he made them wonder just what the difference was between themselves and him.

Raymond soon learned to avoid whites and think of himself as a black. While Raymond was still young, his father turned his mother out of the house where they were living. She began to live with another man, who was black. But this man, Raymond's new stepfather, didn't want to support a white man's children. When Raymond's mother died, he was only 13 years old. He and his sister were thrown out of their home by their stepfather. "Go to the big house and tell your own daddy to feed you," he told Raymond. "I have fed you long enough." These experiences scarred Raymond, but as he grew up he found acceptance among other black people. Many of them were of mixed racial backgrounds themselves. To young Rosa McCauley, it didn't make the slightest difference who Raymond's parents were. He was a charming, gentle, and handsome young man, and she was falling in love with him.

In December 1932, just a few weeks before her 20th birthday, Rosa McCauley married Raymond Parks and took his name. Together they rented an apartment in a black neighborhood of Montgomery and settled down to build a life for themselves. The young Mrs. Parks worked as an insurance saleswoman for a while, but she soon realized that she could earn a better living mending clothes. There was always work for a seamstress. She could either do odd jobs for people at home or work in a store making alterations.

Although Rosa had regular work, Raymond was unhappy that she had given up high school. He himself had had very little schooling because of his difficult childhood. He thought it was a shame that Rosa had to give up school when she had come so close to graduating. He encouraged her to finish her high-school courses, and in 1934 she received her diploma from Alabama State College.

Mrs. Parks was glad to complete her education, but she had

little hope of getting a better job. It had never been easy for African Americans in the South to find good jobs. But it was harder than ever in the years in which Rosa Parks was beginning her married life and finishing her education. These were the years of the Great Depression, in which millions of people lost their jobs. Ever since the stock market crash of 1929, businesses all across the United States had been failing. Thousands of factories, farms, and banks lost money and closed down. Millions of people lost their savings. Families stood on breadlines to get free meals. Unemployed workers roamed the streets in a desperate search for jobs.

Raymond Parks counted himself lucky to have steady work in the middle of the Great Depression. He followed a trade that was always in demand. He was a barber and was never short of work. Raymond had several clients—white men—whose hair he cut at their homes. But he also had a regular job in a barbershop at Maxwell Air Force Base, just outside Montgomery, and that was something to be very glad about. The soldiers and airmen on the base were paid by the government, which meant that they were sure to keep their jobs and get their pay regularly. As long as they did, there would be work for Raymond. His pay wasn't much, but he could count on it. That was more than many people could hope for during the 1930s.

Shortly after Rosa and Raymond were married, Mrs. McCauley came to live with them. Rosa's brother had left Alabama to find work in the North, and Rosa's mother didn't want to live in Pine Level alone. Since they needed more space now, Rosa and Raymond Parks managed to rent a small but comfortable apartment on a newly built block. The only trouble with their home, as the young Mrs. Parks soon realized, was that they were living very close to a white neighborhood. Every evening when she got off the bus after work, she would have to walk past a block of white homes, followed by angry stares and insulting remarks. The white families weren't happy about their new neighbors' skin color. On one occasion, as Mrs. Parks was walking home, a white boy came up behind her and pushed her hard. Rosa Parks wasn't about to take that kind of behavior from anyone, and she pushed the boy back to teach him a lesson. The boy's mother, who had been watching, began screaming at her: "Why did you touch my boy?" and "I'll have you thrown in jail." Rosa Parks knew that blacks had been jailed and beaten for less, but she kept walking. The woman left her alone.

During the depression years, there were fewer of the lynchings and Klan attacks on blacks that had been so common when Rosa Parks was a girl. The old Klansmen were now too busy trying to make a living and keep their families fed. But it also seemed that the hatred many whites felt for blacks had been made sharper by their recent poverty.

One day in May 1931, a fight broke out between black and white youths who had been riding on a freight train in northern Alabama. The young men had been out "junking"—picking up paper and bits of metal at garage dumps to sell. It was hard work, and they made only $3 to $4 a week by selling what they found. Fights often broke out between blacks and whites on the trains that took them from one junkyard to another. This time the blacks drove the whites off the slowly moving train. But when they reached the station at Paint Rock, a police posse went through the train and arrested the riders. Nine young black men, one white man, and two young white women were arrested and locked up in the town of Scottsboro. The next day, to their great surprise, the nine blacks were accused of having raped the two women.

As news of the case spread, few black people believed that the nine "Scottsboro boys" had anything to do with the crime. But they knew that many white people wouldn't wait for the truth before lynching them. They were right. On the day of the trial, 10,000 white men gathered in Scottsboro. It was a strange trial. There were no lawyers to defend the young men, and there was very little evidence. But the court quickly sentenced eight of the nine young men to death. Outside the courthouse, whites celebrated with a band playing the tune "There'll be a hot time in the old town tonight."

Thousands of blacks across the state got together to protest the arrests and to demand fairness in the Scottsboro case. Raymond Parks was one of the first people from Alabama to begin campaigning for the young men's freedom. He did his best to get people in Montgomery to stand behind the Scottsboro boys. The case went to the Alabama Supreme Court in Montgomery. But the judges in the "cradle of the Confederacy" supported the death sentences. The Scottsboro boys were sent to the death house of Montgomery's jail. The same prison held two blacks who had been sentenced to the electric chair for "highway robbery." They had robbed a white man of 50 cents.

Many Americans across the country were shocked at the bloodthirsty racism of the Alabama courts. Several groups worked hard to gather support for the Scottsboro boys. Protest marches were held all over the country. In 1933, Ruby Bates, one of the two women who were supposed to have been raped, joined the campaign to free the prisoners. The authorities seemed to realize that the Scottsboro boys had been sentenced unfairly. None of the death sentences was carried out. In 1937, charges against four of the prisoners were dropped. But the remaining five would wait many years before they were set free. Raymond Parks was very disappointed. It seemed to him that the Scottsboro boys were paying the price for the blind hatred of whites toward blacks.

Meanwhile, Rosa Parks was growing sick and tired of the insults and abuses she faced every day as a black woman in Montgomery. Many years later, when she had left Alabama and made a new life in another state, she remembered her feelings: "Whites would accuse you of causing trouble when all you were doing was acting like a normal human being, instead of cringing. You didn't have to wait for a lynching. You died a little each time you found yourself face to face with this kind of discrimination."

It was on the city buses that Rosa Parks could never forget that she was a second-class citizen in Montgomery. Every day when the bus she caught to or from work arrived, Mrs. Parks and the other black passengers would enter through the front doors and buy a ticket from the driver. Then they would get out of the bus, enter through the rear doors, and look for a seat at the back of the vehicle. The front half of the bus was reserved for whites, and blacks couldn't set foot in it. If the white section was filled, blacks were expected to give their seats to white passengers.

Rosa Parks was finding it more and more difficult to accept this kind of treatment. She would argue with bus drivers who told her to give up her seat, and she would march straight through the front section of the bus after paying her fare. One day in 1943, she was thrown off a bus by a driver named James F. Blake for refusing to use the rear door. Blake told her that if she thought she was too important to go to the back door, she should stay off his bus. Many of the drivers learned to recognize Rosa Parks, with her hair in a braided bun, and her wire spectacles. If they saw her alone at a stop, they would often drive right past her.

Sometimes Rosa Parks wanted to weep at the injustice of segregation, but it would take more than this to stop her. "The most painful thing of all," she said, "was to see little children get on the bus. To them, a seat was a seat, and when they saw an empty one, they sat down. Their mothers would have to snatch them and hurry them to the rear before there was trouble. It was painful to think how they would be taught."

During the 1940s, blacks in Montgomery were being treated more unfairly than usual. Rosa Parks had a good idea why this was so. In December 1941, the United States had entered World War II. Young black men were once again being asked to go abroad to fight for their country. Thousands of them were risking their lives fighting a white enemy. They were winning, too. The whites in Montgomery were glad that the United States and its allies were winning the war, but many of them weren't too happy that black soldiers would share in the victory.

One day passengers on a city bus saw a particularly shocking example of white hatred toward black soldiers. As the bus passed near a Montgomery hospital, the driver had to brake to avoid a young black war veteran who was dancing along the street. The soldier had just been released from the hospital and was a little drunk from celebrating. When the bus driver saw the same soldier again a little farther along the route, he stopped the bus. The driver climbed out and beat the black man with his metal ticket punch. The young man's face bled so badly that he had to be put into the hospital again.

Rosa Parks was furious about the beating. "I went to the trial of the bus driver," she later recalled, "and he was fined $24 for assault and battery, but he didn't leave the job. He continued to drive as usual." This driver was a very heavyset man, weighing more than 200 pounds, while the victim, the young man he attacked, was very thin and frail. He hardly weighed 134 to 140 pounds.

Montgomery's bullying bus drivers made Rosa Parks realize that there was little she could do to change things on her own. After the Scottsboro case, Raymond told her that there was only one organization in Montgomery that was fighting for black people's rights—the National Association for the Advancement of Colored People (NAACP). She decided to find out more about this association.

The NAACP had been established by a group of college-educated blacks and whites in 1910. The association's founders had originally come together to do something about the violence against blacks in northern cities. At its second annual meeting, the NAACP stated that its purpose was "to promote equality of rights" and to put an end to racial prejudice in the United States. During its early years, the organization tried to stop lynchings and other violence against blacks in the South. Its members worked for new laws to punish the lynch mobs that attacked blacks so often in those days.

The NAACP didn't get the laws it wanted passed against lynching. But the organization was winning victories for black people in the courts. In 1915, the NAACP won a Supreme Court ruling that put an end to the hated "grandfather clause." That clause was a law that had prevented many blacks from voting because their grandfathers, who were slaves, hadn't been able to vote. In 1927, the association won another Supreme Court case against the laws that denied blacks their right to vote in the primaries. In the primaries, voters select the candidates who will run in the final elections.

In spite of these and other victories for the rights of black citizens, the NAACP had very few members in the South. But Rosa Parks read about the organization in the pages of its magazine, *The Crisis*. She also heard a great deal about the president of the Alabama branch of the NAACP, Edgar Daniel Nixon, or E. D. Nixon as he was called in Montgomery. Nixon was known as a fearless and tireless man. Apart from his work with the NAACP, he also worked full-time as a porter on the trains that ran from Montgomery to New York City. Railway porters were almost always black men. Nixon was the local leader of the Brotherhood of Sleeping Car Porters, the first black trade union in the country.

In 1943, Rosa Parks went to her first NAACP meeting. Soon she became so active there that E. D. Nixon singled her out as a future official for the local branch of the association. She was one of the first women in the South to join the NAACP. Nixon knew that she was bravely risking the anger of local whites to come to his meetings. After talking to her a few times, he also realized that she had many admirable qualities and made her the secretary of the Montgomery branch of the NAACP.

Suddenly Rosa Parks found herself doing important and satisfying work. As the NAACP branch secretary, she was able to use the many skills and abilities her white employers had ignored. She organized meetings and arranged for guest speakers to visit. She got to know A. Philip Randolph, the founder of the Brotherhood of Sleeping Car Porters, and Roy Wilkins, the national president of the NAACP. As a young woman, Rosa Parks had learned to type perfectly in high school, and she wrote impressive official letters. But she had never been able to find work as a secretary in Montgomery outside the NAACP.

The self-respect that the new job gave her was wonderful, but it was working to destroy segregation that really gave Rosa Parks a sense of purpose. Best of all, she was working with many other good people who were just as determined as she was to put an end to segregation. There were other women fighting segregation in Montgomery and all over the country. She met and often wrote to Ella Baker, a black woman who was the director of the NAACP's youth branch. In Montgomery itself, she knew Jo Ann Robinson, a professor of English at Alabama State College who worked with the Women's Political Council (WPC). The WPC campaigned for better educational facilities and many other basic needs for blacks. She made some white friends, too. Among them were the lawyer Clifford Durr and his wife, Virginia. They were always available if the NAACP needed legal advice, and they became Rosa Parks's good friends.

One of the most important projects Rosa Parks worked on with her new friends and colleagues was the Montgomery Voters' League. For years African Americans in Alabama had been prevented from voting. Even if they were brave enough to ignore the threats of whites and get registered, they faced other problems. Election officials would make blacks take a test of 24 senseless questions to see whether they could read and write. But the officials had been known to fail even the best-educated African Americans. The Voters' League coached people on how to deal with the interviews and how to keep bothering the officials until they registered them as voters. Even after they were registered, new voters had to find money to pay a poll tax. But, as Rosa Parks later recalled, "hardship or not, every Negro who passed found some way to get the money and get his name on the books."

One day Raymond Parks came home from work with some exciting news. Maxwell Air Force Base was being desegregated. On July 26, 1948, President Harry S. Truman signed an order ending segregation in the armed forces. There would be no more segregated washrooms, water fountains, or eating places on the base. Black and white soldiers and airmen would live in the same dormitories and eat at the same tables. But most important of all, it seemed to Raymond, President Truman's order was a clear message that segregation should end.

It looked as though things were beginning to change.

5 STUDENTS OF PROTEST

> ❝ It is to the youth that all of us must look. There is still a great deal for all of us to do, and those who will not dare themselves should certainly support the young people who will. ❞
>
> **ROSA PARKS (cited in the Metcalf Papers)**

Working as E. D. Nixon's secretary, Rosa Parks was able to learn about the struggle for civil rights that was developing across the nation. All sorts of information passed through her hands. There were official letters from the NAACP and the Brotherhood of Sleeping Car Porters, as well as appeals and complaints from private citizens. But while blacks everywhere were sick and tired of being treated like second-class citizens, they weren't uniting to fight the segregation laws that denied them their rights.

There were so many cases of black citizens being crushed by the system while others looked on quietly. Rosa Parks felt frustrated when she thought about this. In Alabama a black man was sentenced to death for stealing $1.95 from a white woman. Another time, right there in Montgomery, a black man was stopped by the police for speeding. He was then nearly beaten to death with a tire iron. During all this, a crowd of black people had simply stood by and watched. Mrs. Parks herself had watched quietly in court as a white bus driver got away with a small fine after beating a black man viciously about the face.

But Rosa Parks wasn't going to watch quietly for very long. That's why she was one of the first women in Montgomery to join the NAACP. She had, in her own words, "almost a life history of being rebellious against being mistreated because of my color." The same rebelliousness sometimes made her do more in her job than a secretary usually does. Nixon would always remember the time when, without asking him, Mrs. Parks wrote a letter strongly criticizing an Alabama politician. She was outraged because the politician had said that the passage of a federal law against lynching would "destroy the peaceful relations between the two races."

There was nothing peaceful about the relations between whites and blacks in Alabama. Black people lived under the threat of white violence every day of their lives. It was only because blacks kept quiet that white politicians could say that the situation was peaceful. They stayed quiet only because they feared the white laws, the white lawmen, and the white lynch mobs. Knowing that a letter signed "Rosa Parks" would probably just be thrown away, she used a sheet of paper with E. D. Nixon's signature on it. The NAACP president didn't find out about the letter he was supposed to have signed until it was already in the mail. He was too surprised to be annoyed with his secretary.

Often it seemed that only the young people still had the spirit to rebel against the injustice that was all around them. In early 1951, Rosa Parks heard of a struggle that had been started by some black schoolchildren in Prince Edward County, Virginia. The teenagers, led by 16-year-old Barbara Johns, had gone on strike because of the terrible condition of their school. For years the school officials had been promising them a new school building. But the education of black children wasn't given much importance in Virginia, and the students had continued to take many of their classes in tar-paper shacks. Finally, they'd had enough. They refused to go to classes until something was done. The students also asked the NAACP to help them. As a result, on May 23, 1951, a month after the strike began, NAACP lawyers filed a suit to end racial segregation in the classroom. At the same time, the lawyers began two other cases against segregated schooling: the *Briggs* case from Clarendon County, South Carolina, and the *Brown* case from Topeka, Kansas. By October 1952, all three cases had moved up to the Supreme Court, which combined them with two others at the last minute and treated them all as a single suit. Because the justices decided to hear the Kansas lawyers first, the combined suit became known as the *Brown* v. *Board of Education* case.

The *Brown* case attracted a lot of attention across the country, and even in the South blacks began to get interested in the NAACP. In the Montgomery branch, the number of members began to grow. One day Rosa Parks typed out a letter of appointment to a new member, Martin Luther King, Jr., who had just joined one of the association's committees. King had only recently moved to Montgomery to begin work as minister of the Dexter Avenue Baptist Church.

The progress of the NAACP's suit in the Supreme Court was a slow business. It would be 1954 before the Court gave its final judgment. But there was a good chance of success, and many people felt encouraged. Young people in Montgomery were also excited about the example that Barbara Johns and the students in Virginia had set. After the strike, the Klan in Virginia had burned a cross in front of Johns's house. This was a warning to her and her family because of the part she had played in the strike. Johns's family then decided to send her away until the whites in Prince Edward County calmed down. She went to stay with her uncle Vernon Johns, a well-known preacher in Montgomery. He had been the minister of the Dexter Avenue Baptist Church for many years before Martin Luther King, Jr., took over the job. Barbara Johns became a familiar face and an inspiration to many young people in Montgomery when she went to stay with her uncle.

Meanwhile, Rosa Parks had begun to work with the NAACP's youth group. Every week the group met in the hall of the Trinity Lutheran Church, which was near the Parkses' home. Robert Graetz, the pastor of that church, was a friend and neighbor of the Parkses. He was also a white minister in a black church and an outcast among Montgomery's whites. They hated him for treating blacks as their equals. The NAACP youth group discussed the history of racial discrimination in the United States. They looked into the most recent developments in the struggle to end it. Often they talked about what they could do to change things. They wanted to challenge the attitudes of whites who thought that blacks must be kept in their place. Parks was very happy to be working with the youth group. She had given up hope that grown-up blacks would do anything to fight segregation. It was the "younger ones," she said, "who were determined not to take it any longer."

The members of the youth group often went into white libraries and tried to borrow books. Sometimes they made a point of sitting in the white section of segregated restaurants or buses. They would almost always be chased away by the librarians, managers, and drivers. But they were making it clear to everyone that they didn't want to live in a segregated world. After these adventures, the excited youngsters would go back and tell Mrs. Parks and their friends about what they had done and how the whites had reacted.

One day when she was working in Nixon's office, Rosa Parks heard that a 15-year-old high-school student, Claudette Colvin, had been arrested for refusing to give up her seat on a Montgomery bus. Colvin was full of spirit. She argued with the bus driver when he ordered her out of her seat. She tried to fight off the police officers before she was taken to the police station in handcuffs. E. D. Nixon thought the NAACP might be able to take up Colvin's case to attack the segregation laws in court. Rosa Parks was thrilled. She still remembered the shame of being thrown off a bus herself. Now, along with Jo Ann Robinson, who had also suffered a bus driver's insults, Mrs. Parks encouraged Nixon to take the case to the federal courts. She believed that the NAACP lawyers could prove to the courts that segregated buses were unconstitutional, just as they were arguing against segregated schools. Parks and Robinson had already begun raising money for Colvin's case and arranging for speakers to support her. E. D. Nixon and Clifford Durr discussed the case with a young black lawyer named Fred Gray, who was eager to represent Colvin in court.

Then came the hitch. It turned out that Colvin was pregnant—and unmarried. For that reason, her mother didn't want her to appear in court. Nixon also decided that it would hurt the African-American cause to use a pregnant teenager to challenge the city administration. The city officials would almost certainly use the fact that Colvin was pregnant to turn people against her. They could make her look like someone who was always getting "into trouble" one way or another. People were already beginning to gossip. The case was given up.

Rosa Parks was deeply disappointed. She felt that Colvin had been made a victim both by the segregation laws and because of her pregnancy. But there was nothing she could do about it. She would just continue working with the youth group and hope that other young people would one day be as brave as Colvin had been.

One day when the group met, Mrs. Parks had some exciting news for them. The Freedom Train was coming to Montgomery. The boys and girls were curious. They had heard of Harriet Tubman, and the Underground Railroad in their group discussions. But what in the world was a Freedom Train in this day and age? Then Mrs. Parks told them about it. The Freedom Train was a real train that was being sent around the country from Washington, D.C., as a lesson in democracy. Inside would be an exhibit of the original U.S. Constitution and the Declaration of Independence. Anyone could go inside for free, and segregation wasn't permitted. Now the Freedom Train was coming to the cradle of the Confederacy, and they could make sure it would be integrated.

The children were eager to carry out Mrs. Parks's new experiment in desegregation. On the day the Freedom Train stopped in Montgomery, they all marched down with her to the railway station. Crowds of white children were already there, and Mrs. Parks and her children just got into line with them. Some of the white teachers were unhappy, but the conductors on the Freedom Train wouldn't allow the white children to be brought in separately. Everyone went in together.

The youth group's visit to the Freedom Train had been a peaceful event. But many white people were furious when they heard what the children and Mrs. Parks had done. Soon the telephone at the Parkses' house began to ring at odd hours of the night. When Mrs. Parks answered, strange gruff voices would mutter threats and shout abuses at her.

Hearing the hate-filled voices on the telephone made Mrs. Parks think of those terrifying nights when she was a child, shivering with fear at the sound of the Tuskegee Klansmen's posses. The galloping hooves had been replaced by the jarring ring of the telephone, but the terror she felt was the same. For 12 years, she had worked with the NAACP to change the way blacks and whites lived together. But had anything changed? Here she was, 42 years old, and still living in fear.

Mrs. Parks was distressed by the threatening calls, but she was even more upset about what had happened to the *Brown* case. In May 1951, the Supreme Court justices ruled that school

segregation was unconstitutional. But instead of forcing the southern states to integrate their schools, the federal authorities chose to leave that job for a later date. Southern politicians, on the other hand, had begun to gather whites to defend segregation.

In July 1954, a new organization was founded to fight for racial segregation and white supremacy—the idea that whites are superior to blacks. It was called the White Citizens' Council (WCC). Unlike the Klansmen, who had an "outlaw" image, WCC members seemed very respectable. They didn't talk about lynchings. They punished blacks who fought segregation by seeing to it that they were fired from their jobs. Often they would try to ruin black businesses by telling white customers to stay away.

The WCC soon became very popular. It held rallies all across the South, and thousands of white families went to them. An ugly mood was spreading. Rosa Parks began to hear stories of brutal attacks on blacks. In 1955, a minister—Rev. George Lee—was killed for helping blacks register to vote in Mississippi. The same year, Emmett Till, a 14-year-old boy, was lynched in Money, Mississippi. His story would go down in history as one of the most gruesome examples of whites' cruelty to blacks.

Emmett, a fun-loving boy from Chicago's South Side, was visiting relatives in Mississippi. He was always playing pranks. Emmett and his cousin Curtis Jones were hanging around a grocery store on a hot summer evening when he pulled a picture of a white girl from his pocket, bragging that she was his girl. Another boy then dared Emmett to speak to a white woman in the store.

Emmett went inside, bought some candy, and said "Bye, baby" to the woman. When an old man heard this and threatened them, the boys sped away to Curtis's grandfather's house.

After three days had gone by, the boys thought they were safe. Then the woman's husband returned from a trucking job

Emmett Till, the 14-year-old boy who was murdered in 1955 for the "crime" of speaking to a white woman.

and word got back to him. According to accounts of what happened, he and his brother-in-law went after Emmett Till. Late one night, Emmett was kidnapped at gunpoint. The kidnappers drove him down to the Tallahatchie River. There they strapped a 75-pound cotton-gin fan to his neck and made him carry it to the river's edge. They ordered him to strip, then shot him in the head. Emmett Till's body was found three days later when the barbed wire with which the fan had been tied to his neck became snagged on a root in the river. One of his eyes had been gouged out, and his forehead was crushed. All of this happened because the boy liked to tease and have fun—and because he was an African American. The next month, an all-white jury in a segregated courtroom found the accused men not guilty of Emmett Till's murder.

6
THE HIGHLANDER SCHOOL

> *At Highlander, I found out for the first time in my entire life that this could be a unified society, that there was such a thing as people of differing races and backgrounds meeting together in workshops and living together in peace and harmony. It was a place I was very reluctant to leave. I gained there strength to persevere in my work for freedom, not just for blacks, but all oppressed people.*

ROSA PARKS (cited in *Eyes on the Prize*)

The telephone calls and the sleepless nights weren't the only price the Parkses paid for the Freedom Train. In the summer of 1955, Raymond Parks's haircutting business also began to suffer as his customers heard about what his wife had done. The fear of whites that Raymond had always felt began to prey on his mind now, leaving him worried and unhappy much of the time.

Rosa Parks felt downhearted over the things that were happening to her family and her life. Apart from the sadness she felt at seeing her husband suffer, and apart from the fear she herself felt, she worried about how they would support themselves if Raymond lost any more customers.

By this time, Rosa Parks was earning only $23 a week at the department store where she worked, and Raymond Parks was making even less. She was always looking out for extra work that she could do at home, mending and stitching other people's clothes. Her friends from the NAACP knew of the difficult position the Parkses were in and tried to help her get enough jobs to make ends meet. E. D. Nixon even arranged for Mrs. Parks to do some sewing for Clifford and Virginia Durr. Virginia Durr knew and admired Rosa Parks, and she felt a little guilty about using the NAACP secretary to do her darning. It was painstaking work, and the Durrs couldn't afford to pay very much, but Rosa Parks needed as much work as she could get. Besides, she enjoyed being with Virginia Durr, who usually sat and chatted with her while they both worked on the clothes. Sometimes Mrs. Durr would go over to the Parkses' house to help Mrs. Parks with the work she took home.

Virginia Durr could understand the fear and the worry that Rosa Parks felt when her family was threatened. The Durrs themselves were hated by most white people in Montgomery because they were friends to many black people and supported the struggle for desegregation. But Virginia Durr knew that no matter how much she and her husband were disliked by the average white person, no real harm would come to them. They had many relatives in the South who were important people. Even if life in Montgomery did become unbearable for them, they would have no trouble getting started again in another part of the country. They had friends in many places, and Clifford Durr could find work as a lawyer almost anywhere.

Rosa Parks had no important relatives to protect her, and nowhere to live but in Montgomery. Slowly but surely, she was being worn down by the threats and the poverty she and her husband were experiencing. Raymond Parks already seemed a broken man to Virginia Durr. She knew that Rosa Parks was a brave woman, but she desperately wanted to do something to help keep her friend's fighting spirit alive during these hard times. Then, one day in April, she had an idea. She would ask Mrs. Parks to visit the Highlander Folk School in Monteagle, a town in Grundy County, Tennessee.

The Highlander School was a place where blacks and whites met for two weeks at a time to discuss the problems of overcoming segregation. During the summer, the school would be holding leadership workshops at its remote camp in the Appalachian Mountains. At these two-week courses, people who were involved in the struggle against racial segregation and inequality discussed how things were going in different parts of the country. At Highlander, they could learn from one another how to organize and lead protests. They could also practice public speaking, and most of all, they could encourage one another. Virginia Durr was convinced that if Rosa Parks spent two weeks there, she would come back filled with courage and hope.

Virginia Durr worked hard to persuade her friend to make the trip to Monteagle. Mrs. Parks worried that she would get new threats from segregationists if she went to the racially integrated workshop. In any case, she couldn't afford to travel. But Virginia Durr told her that no one in Montgomery would know about the trip. She also didn't need to worry about the cost because the course was free. Mrs. Durr then called her old friend Myles Horton, who ran the Highlander School, to ask him to send money for the journey.

By now Rosa Parks had accepted the idea of going, but she still felt it would probably bring her trouble. All the same, maybe she would learn something that would help build up the NAACP youth group. Once everything had been arranged, Virginia Durr drove Mrs. Parks down to Atlanta so that no one in Montgomery would see her boarding a bus to Tennessee. In Atlanta she caught a bus to Highlander.

This was the first break Rosa Parks had had in a long time. She knew it would be awhile before she could take so much time off from work again. The bus was rolling through some beautiful countryside and she wanted to relax and enjoy the trip. But the last few months in Montgomery had shaken her nerves and she couldn't help worrying. She thought she saw some people from Montgomery sitting opposite her on the bus. What if they guessed that she was going to Highlander? If word got around Montgomery, it would mean more threats, more tension. She might even lose her job at the department store. She turned her head slightly and glanced across the aisle to make sure. No, they weren't from Montgomery.

Hours later, when she had arrived at Highlander, Rosa Parks could tell that the next two weeks would be unlike anything she had experienced before. Groups of blacks and whites were chatting and walking around happily with one another. She was shown the room where she would sleep, a dormitory that she would share with five other people. Nearby was a beautiful lake where everyone could go swimming.

At Highlander, Rosa Parks met people who had been fighting segregation openly for years. Myles Horton, a white man and the director of Highlander, had become an outcast among local whites because of his work. Horton had started Highlander in 1932, during the Great Depression. He wanted to help factory workers and miners from the desperately poor Appalachian Mountains to get together and help themselves. But living in Monteagle, Horton grew more and more upset over the distrust and the injustice that separated whites and blacks. Local whites liked to say that no black would dare to spend the night in Grundy County. Myles Horton knew that this kind of fear and hatred were common throughout the South. He decided to do something about it. He began to organize workshops to help people fight racial discrimination.

Highlander soon became especially well known for its literacy workshops. At these workshops, black people who hadn't had much schooling were taught to read and write. They could then pass the literacy tests they needed to take before they could vote. The workshops had brought Horton a lot of hatred from white people who didn't want to see black people being encouraged to vote. But Myles Horton wasn't frightened by his enemies. Instead, he loved to tell amusing stories about his arguments with white segregationists. For Rosa Parks, it was a pleasure to hear him talk:

"Myles Horton just washed away and melted a lot of my hostility and prejudice and feelings of bitterness toward white people, because he had such a wonderful sense of humor. I found myself laughing when I hadn't been able to laugh for a long time."

There were impressive women at Highlander, too. Among them were Septima Clark, a black schoolteacher from Charleston, South Carolina, who had been working to get black people to vote in elections and helping them to pass the literacy tests. It was risky work. Whites would bring their guns out on election day to frighten the new voters. But Mrs. Clark didn't seem to be afraid. At Highlander it is said that she "moved through the different workshops and groups as though it was just what she was made to do."

Rosa Parks felt as if she were just the opposite of Septima Clark. "I was tense, and I was nervous, and I was upset most of the time," she said. The recent months in Montgomery were still fresh in her mind, and she doubted that she could ever be as full of spirit as Clark. She felt that her own spirit "had been destroyed too long ago."

During the day, everyone at Highlander met for the workshops. There they discussed the work they had been doing in many different parts of the country. In the evenings, they gathered in their dormitories to relax, chat, sing, and dance. During most of her stay at Highlander, Rosa Parks had felt too shy to say much. But one evening, people began asking her, "Rosa, how in the world did you deal with that Freedom Train?" Then she began to talk.

"It wasn't an easy task," Parks said. "We took our children down when the Freedom Train came, and the white and black children had to go in together. They wouldn't let them go in otherwise, and that was a real victory for us." Then she shyly told them about her work with the NAACP youth group that she was so proud of and how Virginia Durr had convinced her "to come up here and see what I could do with the same youth group when I went back home."

The next day at the workshop, more people wanted to hear about the Freedom Train, and Rosa Parks told the story again.

But her stay at Highlander was almost over, and she began to worry that people in Montgomery would hear that she was still proud of what she had done and begin harassing her again. When she thought of Montgomery, it was as if she were going back to a life that would never change. At the last workshop, she was asked what she would do when she went home. She had to answer that she didn't think anything would change in her hometown, because most blacks wouldn't stick together. But she promised to keep working with children, to teach them that they had the right to belong to the NAACP and to do things like going through the Freedom Train.

When it was time to leave, Rosa Parks became panicky. What if someone had found out about her weeks at Highlander? She didn't want to take the bus. She was afraid that something might happen. Finally, Septima Clark drove her down to Atlanta and put her on a bus to Montgomery.

Mrs. Parks got back to Montgomery safely. As she began her daily life at home and at work again, she realized that she no longer felt frightened or alone. She remembered all the brave people she had met at Highlander who were fighting for equality and desegregation all across the country.

Three months later, Septima Clark was surprised to hear that her friend, who had been too frightened to take the bus from Highlander, had just been arrested for challenging the bus segregation in Montgomery. "Rosa?" she said. "Rosa? She was so shy when she came to Highlander."

What could have happened?

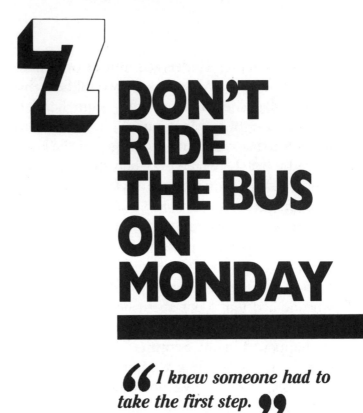

DON'T RIDE THE BUS ON MONDAY

> **❝ I knew someone had to take the first step. ❞**
>
> **ROSA PARKS, to a reporter**

It was Thursday, December 1, 1955. The workday was over, and crowds of people boarded the green-and-white buses that trundled through the streets of Montgomery. Rosa Parks was tired after a full day of stitching and ironing shirts at the Montgomery Fair Department Store. She thought she was lucky to have gotten one of the last seats in the rear section of the Cleveland Avenue bus that would take her home.

Soon the back of the bus was full, and several people were standing in the rear. The bus rolled on through Court Square, where African Americans had been auctioned off during the days of the Confederacy, and came to a stop in front of the Empire Theatre. The next passenger aboard stood in the front of an aisle. He was a white man.

When he noticed that a white person had to stand, the bus driver, James F. Blake, called out to the four black people who were sitting just behind the white section. He said they would have to give up their seats for the new passenger. No one stood up. "You'd better make it light on yourself and let me have those seats," the driver said threateningly. Three men got up and went to stand at the back of the bus. But Rosa Parks wasn't about to move. She had been in this situation before, and she had always given up her seat. She had always felt insulted by the experience. "It meant that I didn't have a right to do anything but get on the bus, give them my fare and then be pushed around wherever they wanted me," she said.

By a quirk of fate, the driver of the bus on this December evening was the same James F. Blake who had once before removed the troublesome Rosa Parks from his bus for refusing to enter by the back door. That was a long time ago, in 1943. Rosa Parks didn't feel like being pushed around again. She told the driver that she wasn't in the white section and she wasn't going to move.

Blake knew the rules, though. He knew that the white section was wherever the driver said it was. If more white passengers got on the bus, he could stretch the white section to the back of the bus and make all the blacks stand. He shouted to Rosa Parks to move to the back of the bus. She wasn't impressed. She told him again that she wasn't moving. Everyone in the bus was silent, wondering what would happen next. Finally Blake told Rosa Parks that he would have her arrested for violating the racial segregation codes. In a firm but quiet voice, she told him that he could do what he wanted to do because she wasn't moving.

Blake got off the bus and came back with an officer of the Montgomery Police Department. As the officer placed Rosa

Rosa Parks is fingerprinted after being arrested for her attempt to integrate the buses.

Parks under arrest, she asked him plainly, "Why do you people push us around?"

With the eyes of all the passengers on him, the officer could only answer in confusion. "I don't know. I'm just obeying the law," he said.

Rosa Parks was taken to the police station, where she was booked and fingerprinted. While the policemen were filling out forms, she asked if she could have a drink of water. She was told that the drinking fountain in the station was for whites only. Then a policewoman marched her into a long corridor facing a wall of iron bars. A barred door slid open. She went inside. The door clanged shut, and she was locked in. She was in jail.

When Rosa Parks was finally allowed to call home, her mother's first question was, "Did they beat you?" Leona McCauley's fears weren't without reason. There had been many occasions when African Americans had been badly mistreated after falling into the hands of the Montgomery police. Rosa Parks hadn't been hit yet, but every minute she spent in jail carried the threat that such a thing would happen.

Frantic with worry, Leona McCauley telephoned the only person she thought could get her daughter released—E. D. Nixon. Nixon's wife answered the phone and heard the story of Rosa Parks's arrest with growing alarm. Her husband wasn't home, but she managed to reach him at his office in downtown Montgomery. Now it was Nixon's turn to panic. He could hardly imagine the quiet, dignified Rosa Parks he knew in prison. Uncertain of what to do next, he tried to call Fred Gray, the young black lawyer with whom he had worked on Claudette Colvin's case. But Gray was nowhere to be found. He then called the jail to ask what crime Rosa Parks had been charged with. The officers were abusive and told him it was none of his business. Finally, Nixon called Clifford Durr. As a lawyer and a white man, Durr had more influence with the authorities. The Durrs were eager to help, and they accompanied Nixon to the jail. Meanwhile, Raymond Parks had also arrived with a friend who had a car. After they deposited $100 in bail with the police officers, Rosa Parks was brought out. She had spent two and a half hours in the cell block.

Leona McCauley, who had been waiting anxiously at home, rejoiced to see her daughter step out of Nixon's car. At least she was out of the hands of the police. The worst that could happen now was that, like Claudette Colvin earlier that year, she would have to pay a fine. The Parkses' home was filled with happy chatter as Rosa Parks described her experience and everyone recalled their reaction to the news of her arrest.

But E. D. Nixon was in a serious mood. He now realized that it was time for the African-American community to make a stand against the unfair bus segregation laws. Rosa Parks had taken the first step, but they would achieve nothing if she just paid a fine. If, instead, she challenged her arrest in court, Nixon felt certain that the case could be taken all the way to the U.S. Supreme Court to win a verdict against segregation. He also thought that Rosa Parks had the dignity and the strength to stand up to the pressures of long days in court. "She wasn't afraid and she didn't get excited about anything," Nixon said. But most of all, he was certain that the black community, which knew and respected Rosa Parks for her work with the NAACP, would stand behind her. He had to ask her.

"Mrs. Parks," he said, "with your permission we can break down segregation on the bus with your case."

Rosa Parks wasn't surprised by Nixon's suggestion, but when her husband heard about it, the terrors of the evening came back to him. "The white folks will kill you, Rosa!" he burst out. But Mrs. Parks had quietly made up her mind that she would fight.

"If you think it will mean something to Montgomery and do some good, I'll be happy to go along with it," she said to Nixon. Rosa Parks had a long battle ahead of her, but she wouldn't be alone.

Late that night, while most of Montgomery slept, several people prepared to defend Rosa Parks and to launch an organized attack on the segregation laws. Fred Gray, who had been out of town, finally received one of Nixon's messages about the arrest. He called Mrs. Parks, and it was decided that he would be her lawyer. Gray then telephoned his friend Jo Ann Robinson, who promptly called a secret meeting of the Women's Political Council (WPC) at Montgomery's Alabama State College.

Long before Rosa Parks's arrest, the WPC had decided to organize a bus boycott to protest the treatment of blacks on City Lines buses. Many of the WPC's members had themselves been insulted by bus drivers and forced to give up their seats in the past. They now drew up a plan to get all of Montgomery's blacks to stop riding the bus as a protest. They knew that without black passengers, the bus company would be crippled. After all, three-fourths of all the passengers on City Lines were black. If they stayed off the buses long enough, the city and the bus company would be forced to treat them better or lose a lot of money. If they could make a bus boycott work, it would change the face of the city. The thousands of black men and women who rode across the city and back again each day would find other ways to go to and from work. The streets would become filled with black walkers and cars. Everyone in Montgomery would notice the change. Perhaps this would make the white people of Montgomery think about segregation.

Rosa Parks's case gave the WPC an opportunity to put their boycott plan into action. Using the college's equipment, they worked through the night to print stacks of flyers to spread the news of Mrs. Parks's arrest. "Another Negro woman has been arrested and put in jail because she refused to give up her seat," the leaflets read. They appealed to blacks not to ride the bus "to work, to school, or anywhere" on the coming Monday.

At three o'clock in the morning, as the printing machines whirred, Jo Ann Robinson called E. D. Nixon to tell him about the boycott plan. The NAACP president had stayed up all night to organize support for Rosa Parks, and he was excited about the WPC's idea. Nixon had been thinking about a boycott, too. He told Robinson that he would arrange a meeting of Montgomery's black leaders to work out the details of the boycott as well as a legal plan for Mrs. Parks's defense.

As day dawned on Friday morning, Nixon called several ministers, including Rev. Ralph Abernathy, the popular minister of Montgomery's largest black church—First Baptist Church—and Rev. Martin Luther King, Jr. He told them about the arrest, the decision to fight the case, and the planned boycott. The ministers were eager to take part in this plan. As they got busy spreading the word, most of Montgomery was setting out for work. Nixon himself had a train to catch. He had to ride a Pullman to New York and back before the day was over. The NAACP president still worked on the railways as a sleeping-car porter.

For Rosa Parks, too, it was just another workday. It rained hard as she took a taxi to the store. Riding in a car, she didn't have to worry about black seats and white seats. But when she reached the department store, the mood was tense. Many of the white people she worked with had heard about her arrest and now treated her with cold silence. Rosa Parks knew that this was just her first taste of the treatment she would have to face from white people. But she hadn't moved for the gruff bus driver yesterday, and she wasn't going to turn around now.

That evening Rosa Parks met with the ministers and other black leaders of Montgomery. They had been very busy during the day. Thousands more leaflets had been printed asking people to stay off the buses and to come to a protest meeting at the Reverend Ralph Abernathy's First Baptist Church on Monday evening. That night volunteers fanned out all over the city. They left the notices in mailboxes, on porches, and in stores for people to pick up. By Saturday, people were talking of little else. Even the white community was alive with stories of the blacks' secret desegregation meetings. On Saturday afternoon, Rosa Parks went to Trinity Lutheran Church for a meeting of the NAACP youth group. Weeks before, she had made arrangements for a speaker to come from Birmingham, Alabama, to tell the children what blacks were doing about segregation in that city. But when she arrived at the church, only a few group members had turned up. Mrs. Parks was surprised. She didn't know that all the others had been busy passing out leaflets about the boycott instead of making plans to come to the meeting.

After she found out what they had been up to, Rosa Parks felt proud of her children. "That's why I love young people so," she said. "There's a time for meetings and a time for speeches—a

very important time—but there is also a time for action, and those young people knew that this was the time for the action and not the speeches."

The next day, on Sunday morning, the pulpits of all the black churches rang with sermons that repeated the message of the leaflets. On Dexter Avenue, on Holt Street, in the Trinity Lutheran Church, and in the Parkses' own St. Paul Methodist Church, the congregations were told that it was their Christian duty to participate in the bus boycott. The fear and worry that

the Parkses had felt on Thursday evening slowly gave way as friends, neighbors, and even strangers promised their support.

As she settled down to sleep that night, Rosa Parks felt exhausted by the events of the past four days. Her trial was to take place the next morning, and she wanted to get a good night's rest so that she would feel fresh for her day in court. But it wasn't easy to fall asleep when she thought about the bus boycott that had turned the entire city of Montgomery upside down.

Only three months earlier, when she was at the Highlander Folk School, Rosa Parks had said that Montgomery blacks wouldn't stick together. Had all that changed?

There was no way of knowing until the next morning.

8 MONDAY MORNING

> *" If we are wrong, the Supreme Court of this nation is wrong. "*
>
>

MARTIN LUTHER KING, JR.

Rosa Parks woke up on the morning of Monday, December 5, thinking about her trial. As she and her husband got out of bed, they heard the familiar sound of a City Lines bus pulling up to a stop across the road. There was usually a crowd of people waiting for the bus at this time. The Parkses rushed to the window and looked out. Except for the driver, the bus was empty and there was no one getting on either. The bus stood at the stop for more than a minute, puffing exhaust smoke into the cold December air as the puzzled driver waited for passengers. But no one appeared, and the empty bus chugged away.

Rosa Parks was filled with happiness. Her neighbors were actually boycotting the buses. She couldn't wait to drive to the courthouse so that she could see how the boycott was going in the rest of Montgomery. When Fred Gray arrived to drive her to the trial, she wasn't disappointed. Rosa Parks had expected some people to stay off the buses. She thought that with luck, maybe even half the usual passengers would stay off. But these buses were just plain empty.

All over the city, empty buses bounced around for everyone to see. There was never more than the usual small group of white passengers in front and sometimes a lonely black passenger in back, wondering what was going on. The streets were filled with black people walking to work.

As Rosa Parks and her lawyer drove up to the courthouse, there was another surprise waiting for them. A crowd of about 500 blacks had gathered to show their support for her. Mrs. Parks and the lawyer made their way slowly through the cheering crowd into the courtroom. Once they were inside, the trial didn't take long. Rosa Parks was quickly convicted of breaking the bus segregation laws and fined $10, as well as $4 for the cost of her trial. This was the stage at which Claudette Colvin's trial had ended seven months earlier. Colvin had had little choice but to accept the guilty verdict and pay the fine.

This time, however, Fred Gray rose to file an appeal on Rosa Parks's case. This meant that her case would be taken to a higher court at a later date. Meanwhile, Mrs. Parks was free to go.

Outside the courthouse, the crowd was getting restless. Some of them were carrying sawed-off shotguns, and the policemen were beginning to look worried. E. D. Nixon went out to calm them, but nobody could hear him in the din. Voices from the crowd shouted out that they would storm the courthouse if Rosa Parks didn't come out safely within a few minutes. When she did appear, a great cheer went up again.

After seeing the empty buses that morning, and this large and fearless crowd around her now, Rosa Parks knew that she

E. D. Nixon, head of the NAACP in Montgomery, shown here with Rosa Parks and her lawyer, Fred Gray.

had made the right decision. Black people were uniting to show the city administration that they were tired of the insults of segregation. Together, they could change Montgomery. They could do some good.

Montgomery's city administration was completely confused by the boycott. Armed police were sent to the bus stops to arrest the troublemakers who they thought must be keeping people off the buses. But the only people who were keeping the buses empty were those who were quietly walking or sharing cars to work, and there were no laws against that. The police officers following the buses succeeded only in scaring away the few black people who hadn't yet heard or didn't care about the boycott.

Later in the afternoon, a small meeting was held to prepare for the protest meeting at the First Baptist Church. The mass meeting was scheduled for 7:00 P.M., but E. D. Nixon and many of Montgomery's black ministers gathered there a few hours earlier to exchange ideas about the boycott and what they should do next.

It was decided that an organization should be established to keep up the fight against segregation. They wondered what they should call the new organization. Someone suggested the Negro Citizens' Committee. But this sounded too much like the White Citizens' Council they all hated. Finally, they agreed on a name. The new group would be called the Montgomery Improvement Association (MIA).

Now that they had a name, the association still needed an official chairman. E. D. Nixon looked at the 26-year-old minister of the Dexter Avenue Baptist Church. He was fairly new in town and had made no enemies in the black community. The young minister had also delivered a fine speech at an NAACP gathering a few months earlier. He would probably make a good chairman. Nixon suggested that Dr. Martin Luther King, Jr., should head the MIA. The other ministers quickly agreed. As the ministers began to discuss the situation, Nixon realized, with rising anger, that they didn't want to take any risks. Their idea of a protest was to pass around more leaflets encouraging the boycott, but without taking a personal stand. None of them wanted their names on the leaflets. They wanted to avoid trouble with the white authorities.

"What you talkin' about?" Nixon demanded. "You guys have went around here and lived off these poor washerwomen all your lives and ain't never done nothing for 'em. And now you got a chance to do something for 'em, you talkin' about you don't want the white folks to know it."

In a fury, Nixon compared the ministers to a bunch of scared boys. Martin Luther King, Jr., the newly appointed chairman of the MIA, wasn't used to taking such insults quietly. He got up and looked at Nixon fiercely. "Nobody calls me a coward," he said. He was willing to support the boycott.

After King's outburst, most of the ministers said they, too, would support the boycott. But as the meeting ended, everyone agreed that they would have to wait and see how the evening meeting went before deciding whether the boycott was a good idea.

E. D. Nixon and the ministers had done all they could do. Now everything depended on the black people of Montgomery. The ministers would have to wait and see whether the black community was willing to carry on the bus boycott. They might not be so enthusiastic at the end of a tiring day when many of them had walked to and from work. There was no guarantee that they would even come to the meeting in large numbers. After all, it would mean another tiring walk to and from Holt Street for most of them.

As the time for the meeting approached, it became clear the church wouldn't be empty that evening. Streams of people began to file in. Before long there was no more room left inside, but the flow of people continued. The crowds began to fill the grounds around the church and spill over into the streets of the neighboring blocks. Loudspeakers had to be set up outside the church so that everyone would be able to hear the speakers inside.

The meeting began with a short prayer. Then Rosa Parks was introduced to the crowd. Everyone inside the church stood up to show their respect for her. Mrs. Parks was surrounded by the cheers and applause of more than 4,000 people, most of whom were standing outside and could not even see her. Only four days earlier, Rosa Parks had been alone in a jail with no one to support her. Now she stood proud, and the entire black community gathered around her.

Several speakers followed Mrs. Parks in addressing the crowd from the church pulpit. Many were powerful preachers. They expressed the feelings of the gathering so perfectly that the

The Reverend Martin Luther King, Jr., became the most popular speaker in the civil rights movement.

crowd shouted in agreement in the middle of many of the speeches. But no one stirred the crowd as much as the young Martin Luther King, Jr. When King took the pulpit, he seemed to speak for all the black people in Montgomery.

King told the meeting that he was glad it was Rosa Parks who had been arrested. "For no one can doubt the height of her character, nobody can doubt the depth of her Christian commitment," he said. "That's right," came the answer from a thousand voices in the crowd.

King waited for silence before he spoke again.

"We are tired," he said, and paused.

"Yes, Lord," the crowd responded.

"We are tired of being kicked around," he continued. "Yes, Lord," the people in the crowd agreed again with anger and determination in their voices.

King spoke of the injustice done to all blacks by Montgomery's segregation laws. He said that it was only right to fight laws that were both unconstitutional and un-Christian.

But despite the anger they all felt, King insisted that they should not react with violence. "The only weapon that we have in our hands this evening is the weapon of protest," he said, and the crowd shouted in agreement. They weren't going to behave like the evil white men of the Ku Klux Klan.

"There will be no crosses burned at any bus stops in Montgomery," King said. "There will be no white persons pulled out of their homes and taken out on some distant road and murdered. [There will be nobody among] us who will stand up and defy the constitution." They would win justice with peace and unity because they were on the side of justice.

"If we are wrong," King told the crowd, "the Supreme Court of this nation is wrong. If we are wrong, God almighty is wrong!" he bellowed. A roar of approval rolled through the crowd.

"We are going to have a real protest," he assured the people. He could see from their faces that they were determined to keep the boycott going until they put an end to segregation. His words echoed that determination.

"We are going to keep walking," King said.

Montgomery's buses were going to stay empty.

THE WALKING CITY

66 We've got to keep on keepin' on, in order to gain freedom. 99

DR. MARTIN LUTHER KING, JR.

As the boycott continued, newspapers from across the country and around the world sent reporters to cover it. Montgomery became known as "the walking city." It was certainly like no other city in the United States. Every morning the streets were filled with walkers. People who once rode the buses together now became marching partners. The bus drivers soon gave up trying to pick up passengers at the stops that had once been packed every morning.

Some of the most determined boycotters in Montgomery were the women. Hundreds of black women who worked as maids and cooks for white families lived some distance from the black neighborhoods. Each morning they would rise earlier than they had ever had to before so they could walk to work and still get there on time. Even so, some of their employers threatened them, demanding that they start taking the bus again if they wanted to keep their jobs. But the women wouldn't give in.

In fact, many white women were so desperate to keep their hardworking maids that they themselves began driving them to work. When the mayor asked white women to stop giving rides to their maids, they ignored him. As one white housewife said, "The mayor can do his own cooking if he wants to, I'm going after my cook."

Of course everyone didn't have an employer who would take them to work, and walking was often out of the question. Many people lived several miles from their workplaces. If they went to work on foot, they would have to spend most of the day marching. At first Montgomery's black taxi services gave rides to carloads of workers at the "emergency rate" of 10 cents each, the same price as the bus fare. But within days after the boycott began, the city's police commissioner killed that plan. He ordered his men to arrest any cab driver who charged passengers less than the regular minimum fare of 45 cents. The city officials wanted to make it more expensive for the boycotters to get to and from work. But the boycotters weren't about to give up their protest.

The MIA leaders came up with their own transportation system. The situation was discussed at one of the church meetings that were being held almost every evening now, and the idea of a community car pool came up. People were excited about the plan. Those who had cars of their own offered them to the pool, while many others volunteered to serve as drivers. By the end of the meeting, a fleet of 150 vehicles was available to drive boycotters to and from work.

It took a great deal of work to keep the boycott going. Rosa Parks had to go to work like most people, but she also spent

The Montgomery Bus Boycott

The Montgomery bus boycott by African Americans of Montgomery, Alabama, lasted from December 5, 1955 until December 20, 1956. The bus company and local merchants lost hundreds of thousands of dollars because of the boycott. African Americans were forced to find some other way around the city through cold and hot weather. Some walked as many as 34 miles a day from the black section of town where they lived to the white section, where they worked, and back. Others used the car pool the black community had organized. Some rode in horse-drawn wagons, and a few rode mules. Their boycott led to an end to the system of segregated buses.

Buses were usually empty during the boycott in Montgomery.

Churches bought station wagons called "rolling churches" to transport the boycotters.

Rev. Martin Luther King, Jr., and Rev. Ralph D. Abernathy were among the first to ride an integrated bus in Montgomery after the Supreme Court ordered an end to segregated buses.

many hours working for the car pool. She helped to draw up timetables and pickup spots for the various routes. The car pool soon had nearly 300 cars transporting 30,000 to 40,000 people a day, and it was running better than the bus company.

Meanwhile, City Lines was paying the price for having mistreated its black passengers for so long. Less than a week after the boycott began, the bus company's officials announced that the company was nearly bankrupt. City Lines was soon forced to discontinue several routes and dismiss many of its drivers. The drivers began to get upset about all the attention they were getting from news reporters. One of them threatened to break a reporter's camera. Another was so unhappy that he said, "I feel like driving this bus straight into the Alabama River."

As for the white passengers who still used the buses, they had to pay higher fares to make up for the money the company was losing because of the boycott. White shopkeepers also felt the effect of the protest, as many blacks stayed away from their stores over the Christmas season.

In spite of all this, white city officials still refused to change the bus rules. Alabama's attorney general himself announced that as far as whites were concerned, "no buses are preferable to integrated buses." In January 1956, the city commissioners tried to trick blacks into going back on the buses. They gave the newspaper a false story saying that they had reached an agreement with the black leaders and that the protest was over. But before the paper with the fake story reached the newsstands, the MIA leaders had heard about the hoax. That night Rev. Martin Luther King, Jr., Rev. Ralph Abernathy, and E. D. Nixon went to all the black bars in Montgomery to spread the word that the boycott was still on. The commissioners' plan failed.

A few days later, on January 24, Montgomery's mayor and one of the commissioners joined the White Citizens' Council. The city's police commissioner had already attended a large rally of the WCC in early January. He promised the crowd of 1,200 whites that he would never give in to the boycotters. He wasn't interested in "a few hundred Negro votes," he told them.

The police commissioner tried to bully blacks into stopping the boycott. Police officers stopped car-pool drivers and gave them tickets for speeding or traffic violations even if they had done nothing wrong. Martin Luther King, Jr., was arrested for speeding and locked up in the Montgomery jail for a few hours. But the arrests and tickets didn't frighten the protesters. Even before the boycott, the Montgomery police had been unfair to black drivers. Although this treatment was worse now, the drivers felt better. They knew the MIA would look after them.

The MIA was still learning to put as much pressure on the city officials as the commissioners had put on the boycotters. During the first two months of the boycott, the black leaders demanded many things from the city. They asked for more black bus drivers and for the white drivers to be polite to black passengers. They wanted to work out a system in which black passengers wouldn't have to give up their seats to whites. But they didn't ask for the buses to be desegregated, even though that was what many blacks wanted. The MIA leadership hoped that desegregation would come through the courts, when they won Rosa Parks's case.

By February 1956, the boycott was in its third month and there was no sign that the city officials planned to give in to any of the MIA's demands. Rosa Parks's case dragged on in Alabama's courts, with no end in sight. The judges kept putting off the date for a new trial. The boycott leaders decided that they had enough. They wanted more than polite bus drivers or more black drivers. They wanted nothing less than an end to segregated buses, and they were going to go on with the boycott until they got it.

There was no point in trying to come to an agreement with the city commissioners or with the Alabama courts. Rosa Parks had gone to court as a defendant, which meant that she was accused of breaking the law. Now her lawyer would open a new case in the federal courts in which the bus company and the Alabama government would be accused of breaking the most important laws in the United States—the principles of the Constitution. In the federal suit, the segregationist lawmakers would be the defendants, or the accused, and the black people of Montgomery would be the plaintiffs, or the people who were filing the suit.

On February 1, Fred Gray filed the papers for the new case in the federal court. That night a bomb was thrown into E. D. Nixon's yard. Fortunately no one was hurt, but it was a signal that the stakes had been raised on both sides. Nor was it just hateful white vigilantes (people who try to take the law into their own hands) who stepped up their attacks. On February 20, the city commissioners and a forum of white businessmen delivered an ultimatum to the MIA leaders. If the boycott was called off, the city leaders said, there would be "no retaliation whatsoever." If it continued, however, they made it clear that the black leaders would be arrested.

The commissioners thought that they could either scare the MIA into giving up the boycott or destroy the protest by jailing its leaders. But while the segregationists were developing their methods of force and intimidation, the African-American com-

Rosa Parks enters the courthouse to continue the legal battle.

munity had found a more effective way of keeping their struggle alive. They called it passive resistance.

Passive, or nonviolent, resistance is a type of protest that was made famous by an Indian leader named Mahatma Gandhi. During the 1930s and 1940s, Gandhi led millions of Indians in a movement to win their country's freedom from Great Britain. While the United States had won its independence by fighting the British, India did the same without a war. Instead, Gandhi's followers boycotted British products and held huge but peaceful rallies and marches. When the British authorities sent policemen to arrest protesters, the Indians offered to fill the jails. When the policemen beat them, they refused to fight back.

When black people in Montgomery heard about Gandhi's protest movement, they were impressed. In many ways—from Rosa Parks's encounter with the bus driver to the entire community's boycott—passive resistance seemed to come naturally to them. But as they began to take their peaceful protest more and more seriously, blacks also had to give up some things they had always counted on—shotguns, for example. It wasn't unusual for black men in Montgomery to have guns. They brought them out proudly to protect Rosa Parks on the day she went to court. Some of the ministers' houses even had armed guards. Now they decided that it was wiser to lock their guns away.

The boycott leaders discussed the city commissioners' latest threats. They realized that if they followed Gandhi's example and went to jail together, they would be able to embarrass the authorities and preserve their unity at the same time. They would refuse to cooperate with a system that mistreated them. But at the same time, they would demonstrate their willingness to experience great hardship for what they believed was right— and they would do so without resorting to violence.

The boycott leaders informed the commissioners that they would not give in.

PAYING THE PRICE

" Montgomery today is nothing at all like it was as you knew it last year. It's just a different place altogether since we demonstrated. "

ROSA PARKS, 1956

A few days later, on February 22, 1956, E. D. Nixon marched into the sheriff's office in the county courthouse. "Are you lookin' for me?" he asked the sheriff. "Well, here I am." He then invited the officers to arrest him as a leader of the boycott. Surprised, the police officers quietly booked, fingerprinted, and photographed Nixon. Then they released him after he gave them a bond of $300. But the officers would have a lot more work to do that day. No sooner had Nixon left the station than a smiling Methodist minister walked in and asked to be arrested. Throughout the day, a stream of

people marched into the sheriff's office and demanded the same treatment.

Rosa Parks was among them, and she was struck by the difference between this occasion and her first arrest only two months earlier. When the police came for her that day, none of the black people on the Cleveland Avenue bus had said one word to defend or even to express sympathy for her. But "this time," she was delighted to see, "we were surrounded by crowds of people, and reporters and photographers [from] all across the country were on hand. We had such a spirit of unity that there were people who felt somewhat left out when they were not among those arrested."

More than 80 well-known boycotters were arrested that day, and each one emerged smiling after leaving a bond with the police. As a crowd of several hundred blacks cheered, the sheriff got upset. He rushed out and shouted, "This is no show!" He knew that the boycotters had made the authorities look ridiculous. The blacks weren't scared of being arrested or of going to trial, though.

The next day what happened was in newspapers all over the world. Readers everywhere were shocked at the news from Montgomery. Even people who didn't support the boycott thought the city commissioners had gone too far. The editor of Montgomery's own newspaper, the *Advertiser,* called the mass arrests "the dumbest act that has ever been done in Montgomery." The boycotters were happier than ever.

Rosa Parks was now involved in two court cases. There was the original case stemming from her arrest on the bus. And now, following the mass arrests, she was charged with taking part in an illegal boycott. But she didn't worry about them much. She knew that the blacks of Montgomery were sharing the responsibility of fighting segregation.

Rosa Parks was devoting even more time to the boycott work now. Along with Martin Luther King, Jr., Ralph Abernathy, and the other MIA leaders, Parks was traveling around the country to raise support for the protest. She was a speaker at many fund-raisers where money was collected to keep the Montgomery car pool on the road. She went to Washington, D.C., as the guest of a black women's organization there, and to Los Angeles to speak to the local branch of the NAACP. On these fund-raising tours, she visited many other NAACP branches, as well as church groups, in New York and in Boston and Springfield, Massachusetts. Mrs. Parks also went back to the Highlander Folk School to speak at a workshop about what was happening in Montgomery.

At the start of the boycott, money had been one of the biggest problems for the MIA. But as the protest continued, its members collected so much from supporters all over the world that the car pool was able to buy more than 15 new station wagons. In order to avoid legal problems with the city's transportation laws, the new cars were registered in the name of Montgomery's black churches. They also had large crosses painted on them and were soon known as the "rolling churches." As for the high costs of the many court cases, the NAACP had decided to pay for the boycotters' legal expenses.

In Rosa Parks's personal life, however, there was a different price to pay. Five weeks after the boycott began, she lost her job. Montgomery Fair Department Store informed her that the alteration shop where she worked was being reorganized. It wouldn't be needing her anymore. With all the work that needed to be done for the boycott, she would still keep busy. But she began to realize that it wouldn't be easy to find a new job in Montgomery. Rosa Parks had become too much of a symbol of the boycott. Anyone who employed her would do so at the risk of losing business from white patrons.

Raymond Parks's business also began to suffer for similar reasons. The boycott was turning into a nightmare for him. He had worried from the start that his wife would earn the hatred of Montgomery's whites. Now what he feared was really happening. They had both lost their jobs, and all day long their phone rang with hateful white callers. Rosa Parks would never forget these calls. "They would say I should be beaten or killed because I was causing so much trouble," she later recalled. "And then there were some who called to inquire whether I had lost my job and when I finally did, I remember one person saying she was sorry and then laughing before she finally hung up." Raymond Parks knew that their enemies could do much worse things to them. Bombs had already been thrown at the homes of E. D. Nixon and Martin Luther King, Jr. Their own home might be next. With all the stress, Raymond Parks became ill and had a nervous breakdown.

Just as things were looking their bleakest in the Parkses' home, however, some wonderful news reached Montgomery. On June 4, 1956, federal judges reached a decision in the anti-segregation case that the MIA had been fighting. By a two-to-one vote, the three judges had ruled that the bus segregation laws were unconstitutional. The lawyers for the city of Montgomery and the state of Alabama immediately appealed the case. This meant that it would now go to the Supreme Court. That was just what the boycotters wanted. If the Supreme Court justices agreed with the federal judges, it would mean the end of segregation on buses.

But what if the judgment went against the protesters? They could only count on the skill of their lawyers and the good sense of the judges—and wait.

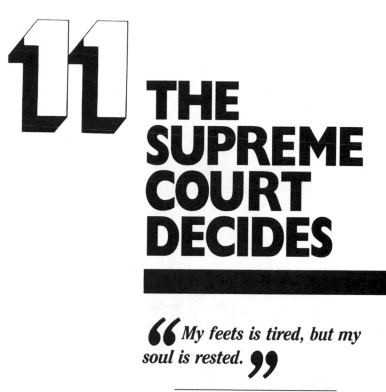

11
THE SUPREME COURT DECIDES

66 *My feets is tired, but my soul is rested.* 99

SISTER POLLARD, an elderly
Montgomery boycotter

O n Tuesday, November 13, 1956, Martin Luther King, Jr., sat at the defendant's table in a Montgomery courtroom. The city officials had come up with a new scheme to destroy the MIA. King listened nervously as the city lawyers argued that the protesters' car pool was nothing but a private business that hadn't paid any taxes. They asked the judge to ban the car pool and fine the MIA $15,000 for unpaid taxes. It looked as though the judge was convinced. He said he would make his ruling after a short break.

King stayed in the courtroom, waiting for the decision. As he waited, a man walked up to him and slipped something into his hand. It was a news bulletin, fresh from one of the ticker machines from which reporters got all the latest news. King couldn't believe his eyes as he read the news. The U.S. Supreme Court had finally made its ruling, confirming the earlier decision of the federal district court. Segregation on public transportation in Alabama was illegal. The judges were so sure of their opinion that they hadn't even bothered to hear both sides of the argument in the case. The Court simply announced that "the motion to affirm is granted, and the judgment is affirmed." The Court had agreed with (affirmed) the MIA's demand (motion) that the federal district court's earlier judgment was right. King ran to the back of the courtroom to tell his wife,

Coretta, his friend, Rev. Ralph Abernathy, and E. D. Nixon. The room buzzed with whispers as the news spread. Finally, a black man stood up and said loudly, "God Almighty has spoken from Washington, D.C.!"

The judge had returned by this time. He tried to silence the courtroom as he delivered his own verdict against the MIA. But nobody cared about fines now. They wouldn't need the car pool anymore. They would be back on the buses.

Montgomery's blacks were jubilant. For 11 months they had shared the same struggle, and now they had won. African Americans throughout the city looked forward to their first rides in desegregated buses. There would be no more crowded "rolling churches," no more tiring walks across town. They

Right after segregation on public buses was declared illegal, blacks and whites ride a Birmingham bus.

planned to ride the buses to work on Wednesday. But just as the MIA leaders were about to call off the boycott, they discovered that the buses wouldn't be integrated for some time yet. Montgomery officials had filed a legal request known as a petition, asking the Court to take back the judgment. Until the judges replied to the petition, the buses would stay segregated. It was a great disappointment, just when so many people were on the point of celebrating. The MIA held a mass meeting to explain the delay. It was decided that the boycott would continue until the final ruling came down from the Supreme Court and the buses were actually desegregated.

At last, on December 20, 1956, Montgomery's segregation laws were officially ended. The next day, buses roared into the African-American neighborhoods to pick up their first passengers since the boycott began. Many of the drivers had been forced off the buses by the boycott. Because the bus company lost so much money, many of them had been laid off without pay during the protest. Now they realized that they owed their work to their black passengers and welcomed them back with smiles.

A pack of reporters went over to the Parkses' home that day. They followed the woman who had started it all one day. The last time she had been on one of the buses—in December 1955—she was part of a full load of segregated passengers. Her first desegregated bus was quite empty, but as the cameras clicked, she heard a white woman complaining about the publicity. She realized then that it would be some time before all of Montgomery's whites could accept the change. But for the moment, Rosa Parks was going to enjoy the ride. All she would say, with her usual shyness, was, "It was quite interesting to be on the bus again." Yet the simple, boxlike vehicles, rattling down the streets of Montgomery, must have felt like luxurious limousines to those first black passengers. They could get in at the front, stroll down the aisle to the back if they wanted to, or sit down in the very first row.

All over town that day, black women, men, and children took joy rides in the city buses. As they sat back on the stiff benches, they thought about the boycott and all they had been through during the past 12 months. They had walked in the cold and the rain, and had spent long hours in car-pool lines.

Women remembered the pride they had taken in walking to work together. White people would never forget it either. As one white woman said, "The real power of the boycott was the Negro women. Every morning they came by our door here. It was like watching a brook to look out and see them going by steadily for an hour or so every morning and an hour or so every evening."

Car-pool drivers remembered being ticketed by the Montgomery police. Many people remembered watching the mass arrests outside the sheriff's office. Others remembered being arrested. But every last one of them remembered the spirit of the mass meetings during the boycott—the sound of a preacher's voice rising and falling, and the thundering replies of a thousand voices of people who knew they could trust one another to keep walking until they won. They had all won.

THE SEGREGA- TIONISTS FIGHT BACK

> **❝ I would rather die and go to hell than sit behind a nigger. ❞**
>
> **A white Montgomerian's reaction to the Supreme Court's decision**

For the first few days after the Supreme Court's decision reached Montgomery on December 20, it seemed as though Montgomery's whites would accept integration peacefully if not as happily as the city's blacks had achieved it. Then the city administration spoke. In a public announcement, the commissioners stated that they had no choice except "to bow to the Court's decision." But they swore to fight to bring back segregation in public transportation. They also warned blacks that unless they accepted segregation on and off the buses, there would be bloodshed.

To many African Americans, it sounded as if the commissioners were threatening them. When the MIA requested that the authorities put police escorts on the buses at night, nothing was done. But officials made public predictions that there would soon be violence over the issue of the desegregated buses. Blacks began to suspect that the city officials wanted to see trouble on the buses. For the commissioners, any violence would be proof that "integration doesn't work." There were many white people from Montgomery who would be glad to give them that proof.

As if in answer to the authorities' prediction, on December 26, two buses were fired upon by hidden gunmen. Two days later, a bus was fired at twice in the same evening. A young pregnant black woman was hit in the legs. By December 29, five buses had been fired upon. On Christmas Eve, a young black girl was waiting alone at a Montgomery bus stop when a car pulled up. Five white men got out of the car, beat her, and then roared off. Instead of trying to catch the white men who had been committing these crimes, the city administration suspended bus service after five o'clock. Many people still remembered the Alabama attorney general's words during the boycott. No buses were preferable to integrated buses, he had said. It looked as if the gunmen and the commissioners had decided that there would be no buses.

As the new year, 1957, began, full bus service started again. But only two days later, a white gunman again opened fire on a bus. After suspending evening bus service again for a few days, the city officials made a public announcement in which they said they would take no special measures to prevent or stop the violence. Again, it seemed to many people that the officials were trying to encourage more violence. And once again, there was violence. Another bus was fired at, and service was suspended for the third time.

Soon the violence began to spread beyond the buses. During the first hours of Thursday, January 10, a group of white men drove around Montgomery's black neighborhoods with a car filled with sticks of dynamite. From time to time, the car slowed as it drew up to a church building or someone's home. The men inside then threw out a bundle of dynamite and sped off. As the car sped through the Parkses' neighborhood, two of the bundles were thrown near the home and church of their friend, the Reverend Robert Graetz. The fuses on the dynamite sticks sparked and burned for a few minutes. Then there was a huge blast. Buildings were torn apart, cars parked on the street were destroyed, and people began to shout with fear.

Rosa and Raymond Parks were awakened by the sound of the explosion. They pulled on their coats and rushed to see if their friends and neighbors were safe. Despite his recent illness, Raymond Parks led a small group of friends into the blocks where the bomb had gone off. When they got to the Graetzes' parsonage, they found it a shambles, with the front destroyed and window frames hanging out. Fortunately, no one had been hurt. But as Mr. Parks looked around the block, he found another bundle of dynamite. The fuse was still smoldering, but another neighbor quickly cut it off. As soon as they were sure of the Graetzes' safety, Rosa and Raymond Parks helped clear the rubble.

Four black churches were bombed that night, as well as the homes of Rev. Ralph Abernathy and Rev. Robert Graetz. Two days later, the white bombers had another busy night. They blew up the office of a black taxi company and another home. They also left 12 smoldering sticks of dynamite on the porch of Dr. Martin Luther King, Jr.'s, home. But these were found just in time to be put out. As a result of the bombings, the city stopped bus service altogether. For an entire week, whites as well as blacks had to find their own way of getting to work.

The city commissioners seemed to realize that unless they did something to stop the violence, nobody in Montgomery would be able to lead a normal life. Seven white men were suddenly arrested and charged with several of the bombings and

Ralph Abernathy (right) walks with Martin Luther King, Jr. (center), during the bus boycott.

shooting attacks. Although two of these men confessed to throwing the bombs, the white jurors found them not guilty. The judge set them all free. While white segregationists were happy to see the men free, the trial also marked the end of the bombings and the attacks on buses. White people were happy to see that in the courts at least, they were still treated better than black people were. The blacks could have their integrated buses, they seemed to think. But as long as whites controlled the city's courts, everything else would stay segregated.

Of course black people weren't going to give up the struggle for integration and equality. But it was good to finally enjoy their victory in peace. Normal bus service had begun again even in the evenings, and there were no more white gunmen waiting in the bushes for the chance to shoot at a bus. People in Montgomery began to get used to the results of the struggle that Rosa Parks had started. But she was still paying a sad price for her courage. She had lost her main job many months earlier, and now that the boycott was over, she had no work with the MIA either. She couldn't find another job. Most of the jobs in Montgomery were controlled by white bosses, and they wouldn't hire her. Even if they didn't hate her themselves, they were afraid of losing white customers if they employed her.

Raymond Parks had also been without a job for many months. Most of his customers didn't want to have their hair cut by the husband of Rosa Parks. In any case, ever since his nervous breakdown, he wasn't really able to work—at least not in Montgomery. The violence and threats that came after the Supreme Court's decision had done nothing to calm Raymond Parks's shattered nerves. With Leona McCauley ill most of the time, the family's situation seemed desperate.

The movement that had been shaped by the bus boycott didn't disappear when the boycott ended. In February 1957, in Atlanta, a group of preachers established the Southern Christian Leadership Conference (SCLC) to carry on the struggle against segregation. Martin Luther King, Jr., had been elected president of the new movement. But Rosa Parks knew that the people with whom King worked had trouble accepting the fact that ordinary women like herself could play an active role in political struggles. They mockingly referred to her as "an adornment of the movement," as if she had only played a symbolic role in the boycott.

In fact, Martin Luther King, Jr., had become so famous as the leader of Montgomery's blacks that people sometimes forgot all the other important figures who had helped to bring about the boycott. E. D. Nixon felt the sting of this and told a story that expressed his feelings:

"I was on an airplane coming down from New York some time ago, sitting beside a lady, and she asked who I was, and I told her. She said, 'Oh, you're down in Montgomery, Alabama.' She said, 'Lord, I don't know what'ud have happened to the black people if Rev. King hadn't went to town.'

"I said, 'If Mrs. Parks had got up and given that man her seat, you'd never heard of Rev. King.'

"When I said that, man, I as well as spit in her face."

Nixon grew so tired of being ignored by King's friends and supporters in the MIA that he resigned from the organization he had helped to start. He was tired of being "treated as a child."

The treatment Rosa Parks received wasn't much better. But right now, the situation at home was so desperate that she had to turn her mind away from the desegregation movement and think about her family's survival. She had to find some way to make a living, but it was beginning to look as though that would be impossible in Montgomery. Finally, she decided that they would leave Alabama and join her brother, Sylvester McCauley, in Detroit, Michigan. For many years, blacks who had grown tired of the hardships of life in the South had been moving to Detroit. Detroit blacks had been able to put a black congressman in office. Rosa Parks remembered Charles C. Diggs, a black congressman from Detroit who had come down to Montgomery for the boycott trial. He brought a large sum of money that people in Detroit had collected to support the protest. There was no doubt that "up north," as people said, blacks could lead a freer life. With a little luck, they could get a job working for a big corporation instead of for some white man who thought he owned them. Sylvester McCauley himself had a steady job working for the Ford Motor Company.

In December 1957, Rosa Parks and her small family boarded a train for Detroit. They would never live in Montgomery again.

13 THE CIVIL RIGHTS MOVEMENT

> 66 *I'm in favor of any move to show that we are dissatisfied. We still haven't received our rights as citizens.* 99
>
> **ROSA PARKS, speaking after the Montgomery boycott**

Sylvester McCauley was waiting at the train when his sister and the rest of the family arrived in Detroit. As he drove them back to his home, Rosa Parks must have felt like a stranger in a new land. The car crawled along the streets beneath tall office buildings and enormous housing projects. The "projects" were huge apartment buildings that the city had built to provide cheap housing for Detroit's growing population. The enormous red brick apartment blocks couldn't have been more different from the traditional two-story wooden homes of Montgomery. The weather was cold and gray. Snow covered the streets. Rosa Parks wondered what sort of life this new city would offer them.

Detroit certainly had its own problems. People here weren't hemmed in by segregation laws, but there were many things that reminded Rosa Parks of the South. Although Detroit's population was mostly black, the city administration was run by whites. Black and white children didn't go to the same schools. Housing was just as segregated here as it was in Alabama. A black person thought twice before walking through a white neighborhood. Rosa Parks could see that more than the law would have to be changed before African Americans could hope to be treated like full citizens of this country.

On August 29, 1957, eight months after the Parkses left Montgomery, the United States Congress passed a civil rights bill. This was done to make sure that black people had the same rights that white citizens enjoyed. In fact, though, the bill gave them very little. According to the new law, government officials who prevented blacks from voting could be punished by law. But blacks had seen the law at work in the trial of the Montgomery bombers. They knew that almost any southern official who was arrested under the new law would be set free by a white jury. The new law also did nothing to force the southern states to integrate their schools.

Most African Americans felt disappointed by the new law, and some felt that they would be better off without it. But many important black leaders, including Martin Luther King, Jr., thought the law was better than nothing. All the same, they now knew that black people would get their full rights as citizens—their civil rights—only through their own actions. The Montgomery bus boycott had shown them that through protest, they could change the segregation laws and their own lives. Now such black organizations as the NAACP and the SCLC were ready to put the lessons of Montgomery to work all over the South.

At the same time, many white politicians had decided that

they would have to crush the desegregation movement before it grew too strong. Several southern governors accused the NAACP of being a Communist organization. During the 1950s, most Americans had a great fear of communism, which many believed was a Russian plot to destroy the United States and take over the world. The governors decided to use this fear against the desegregationists. They called for special meetings of their state assemblies to look into the NAACP.

The state assemblies demanded to see the NAACP's membership lists. The organization refused to show them. The NAACP feared that white politicians would give the lists to such racist groups as the Klan and the WCC. Now, however, the state governments could use the NAACP's refusal to outlaw the organization. Within six months in 1956, all NAACP branches in Louisiana, Texas, and Alabama had been closed. The youth groups with which Rosa Parks had spent so many happy hours in Montgomery would not meet again.

The NAACP wasn't the only antisegregation organization to come under attack at this time. The Highlander Folk School also came under investigation for "Communist activities." The Tennessee attorney general began looking for an excuse to close the school.

In spite of these new problems, African Americans weren't going to give up their struggle. In September 1957, NAACP lawyers won an important victory when the federal courts forced Central High in Little Rock, Arkansas, to accept nine black students. The governor there resisted and ordered the National Guard to the school. The first time one of the black students approached the school, her path was blocked by a National Guardsman. Then she was chased away by a raging crowd of white people who spat on her and shouted, "Lynch her, lynch her!" For days the crowd gathered in front of the school to keep the black students out. In the end, the federal government had to send soldiers to protect the Little Rock Nine, as the students came to be called. But by the last week in

September, they began to attend Central High. It was a small but important victory against segregation.

Meanwhile, Rosa Parks now had an old friend at the SCLC—Ella Baker. Ella Baker had been the director of the NAACP's youth branches when Rosa Parks was organizing one of those branches in Montgomery, Alabama. Unlike Mrs. Parks, she didn't have a family to care for, so she was able to devote all of her time to civil rights work.

Rosa Parks also had another friend on the SCLC's staff—Septima Clark. Like Ella Baker, Septima Clark was a single woman who lived for the movement. Still, she wasn't always happy about the way she and other women in the SCLC were treated. "Dr. King didn't think too much of the way women would contribute," she complained. "But in those days, of course, in the black church, men were always in charge. It was just the way things were."

But things were changing. Ella Baker had started a project called the Crusade for Citizenship to encourage blacks to vote in the South. With Clark's help, she planned to bring more women into the "crusade" to get blacks back on the voting registers. Whites had always made it difficult for blacks to get their names on the lists—known as "registers"—of voters. Now the SCLC took large groups of people to be registered at the same time so no one would be threatened and forced to give up.

The SCLC worked to strengthen voting rights. Many young people who had been inspired by the Montgomery boycott began to wonder what they could do to carry on the struggle against segregation. On Monday, February 1, 1960, four college students in Greensboro, North Carolina, decided to break the segregation laws at a lunch counter in that city. The laws allowed blacks to shop in stores, but not to rest and have a snack at a lunch counter after their shopping. The four students sat for several hours at the whites-only counter without being served. But as word got around, they became heroes by the end of the day. Two days later, 63 people crowded the same lunch counter

This white lunch counter closed when black sit-in protesters waited to be served.

in a sit-in protest against segregation. By Friday of that week, more than 300 people were involved in the sit-ins.

Sit-in protests quickly became a regular event in many southern towns. Often both black and white students sat at the counters together until they were all served. More often, the protesters were attacked by white customers who poured sugar, ketchup, and hot coffee over them. Sometimes they were beaten and thrown out or even arrested. But the protesters never fought back, and the arrests always encouraged more sit-ins.

In March 1960, Septima Clark organized a workshop at Highlander to gather student protesters from across the South.

But the students were also trained for voter registration work and for lunch-counter sit-ins. It was the last workshop that would be held at the school. Later that year, the authorities closed Highlander and auctioned off all its land and property.

But there was nothing the authorities could do to stop the civil rights movement. In April, a second student conference was set up by Ella Baker at Shaw University in Raleigh, North Carolina. The student representatives formed an organization of their own. In Atlanta, that May, they formally named their organization the Student Nonviolent Coordinating Committee (SNCC). Soon the SNCC had thousands of young people involved in antisegregation protests and voter registration work.

News of all these struggles—the Little Rock Nine, the Crusade for Citizenship, and the sit-ins—appeared in newspapers across the country. As a result, although Rosa Parks was far from her old home as the 1960s began, she knew that something important was happening in the South. She remembered the days when she was so sure that southern blacks would never get together, and she had to smile to herself. She was glad she had been wrong.

The new spirit among blacks was so strong that white politicians began to think about what they called "the Negro vote." The year 1960 was a presidential election year, and it promised to be a close race. President Dwight D. Eisenhower was about to retire, and his vice president, Richard M. Nixon, was running as the Republican candidate. The Democratic party's candidate was John F. Kennedy, a popular young senator from Massachusetts. Kennedy tried to win the support of black leaders and black voters before the election. He promised to pass new civil rights laws if he was elected. When Martin Luther King, Jr., was illegally imprisoned a few days before the election, Kennedy helped to get him out of jail. Kennedy won the election and became the new president of the United States. The work against racism and segregation in the South continued.

One of the buses used by Freedom Riders was fire-bombed by a mob of whites outside Birmingham.

In May 1961, another organization—known as the Congress of Racial Equality (CORE)—organized a form of protest known as the Freedom Rides. On the Freedom Rides, groups of people—both black and white—went on a tour of the states in the South. This wasn't a new idea. As early as 1946, the Supreme Court had ruled that integrated seating on interstate buses—buses traveling from one state to another—was legal. CORE then decided to see whether integrated seating on trips between states was really possible. The first Freedom Riders went south in 1947 and were sent to jail in North Carolina for breaking the state's segregation laws. When the new Freedom Riders of the 1960s arrived in some of the large cities of the Deep South, they were met by violent crowds who beat them severely. A Freedom Ride bus was actually burned by such a crowd near Anniston, Alabama, and when the Freedom Riders reached Montgomery, they faced a particularly brutal beating. They were in so much danger that the United States government had to send federal marshals to Montgomery to protect them.

The Freedom Riders never fought back against their attackers, but they never gave up either. Bruised, bloody, and

bandaged, they traveled on through the South in high spirits. As they neared Jackson, Mississippi, one of the riders began to sing a song:

I'm taking a ride on the Greyhound bus line.
I'm riding the front seat to Jackson this time.
Hallelujah, I'm travelling;
Hallelujah, ain't it fine?
Hallelujah, I'm travelling
Down Freedom's main line.

The riders weren't attacked in Jackson. Instead, they were taken straight to jail. But they had already shown the government what a terrible thing segregation was. By September, segregated bus travel had been banned.

The next year, 1962, the government had to send federal marshals to the South again. This time they went to protect just one man, James Meredith. Meredith wanted to study at the University of Mississippi (better known as "Ole' Miss"), and his grades were good enough to get him in. The only problem was that he was an African American. When he was refused admission, Meredith took the university to court with the help of the NAACP. The federal courts ordered the university to admit Meredith, but when he went there, he was turned away by the governor of Mississippi himself. In the end, federal troops had to fight off hundreds of rioting white students before Meredith could begin studying at the university.

In September 1962, while Meredith was still trying to get into Ole' Miss, Rosa Parks went south to Birmingham, Alabama, for the SCLC's convention. Birmingham was known as the most segregated city in the country. Lunch counters were "for whites only," schools were segregated, and blacks were often attacked in the streets by white gangs. In May 1961, the city police had stood and watched as a white mob beat up the Freedom Riders who had just arrived there. But Rosa Parks and the 300 other SCLC members who went to the convention had a peaceful stay—until the last day.

That day Martin Luther King, Jr., was speaking to the SCLC members in a packed church hall when a white man walked up to him and hit him on the jaw with all his might. Rosa Parks looked on in horror as the man went on hitting King. But when the furious crowd jumped up and grabbed the attacker, King shouted, "Don't touch him! Don't touch him! We have to pray for him."

The attacker wasn't harmed by anyone in the church, but the Birmingham priest arrested him. He turned out to be a member of the American Nazi party. King was all right except for a swollen jaw and a headache. Rosa Parks gave him a cola drink and an aspirin to stop the pain. But everyone was proud that they hadn't become violent.

The very next year, in 1963, Birmingham would see plenty of violence. The SCLC went to the city to organize a protest march by black children. On May 2, the police arrested 959 children who had taken part in the protest. The next day more than 1,000 children stayed out of school to march downtown for a protest meeting. The children didn't get very far before the Birmingham police appeared and set huge dogs on them. Then the city firemen blasted the children with fire hoses. The jets of water from the hoses were so strong that the children were knocked down and sent flying against trees and parked cars. It was a horrifying sight, but thanks to TV cameramen it was seen by people around the world. These wild scenes went on for several days, with the protests growing larger and the police making mass arrests in between their fire-hose attacks. As the children were led away, they danced and sang a freedom song to the tune of "The Old Grey Mare":

I ain't scared of your jail
'cause I want my freedom!
. . . want my freedom!

Two hundred fifty thousand people joined the 1963 March on Washington to demand civil rights for all.

As a result of the children's protest in Birmingham, the city's business leaders and store owners promised to desegregate lunch counters and hire black workers for jobs that had been open only to whites until now. Integration was coming to the most segregated city in the country.

All the same, the struggle wasn't over. Many people were disappointed with President Kennedy. He had already been the president for three years, and he still had to keep his promise to have new laws passed that would protect the civil rights of African Americans. In June 1963, Kennedy finally presented Congress with a new civil rights bill. If Congress accepted the bill, it would go back to the White House for the president's signature. It would then become a new Civil Rights Act, a law much stronger than the one that had been passed in 1957. This law would allow the government to sue school boards that refused to become integrated, and it would put an end to the segregation of public places.

Black leaders and civil rights groups decided to organize a march and a meeting in Washington to show Congress that they wanted a new Civil Rights Act. In August 1963, as TV cameras looked on from atop the Washington Monument, more than a quarter of a million people gathered in front of the Lincoln Memorial for the largest mass meeting of the civil rights movement. The crowd stood for three hours as they were introduced to leading figures in their long struggle for justice. Rosa Parks was there, along with many other people who had taken part in the Montgomery boycott. But the March on Washington would be best remembered for the last speech of the day, which was given by Martin Luther King, Jr.

In this speech, "I Have a Dream," King spoke of the day "when all God's children, black men and white men, Jews and Gentiles, Protestants and Catholics, will be able to join hands and sing in the words of the old Negro Spiritual, 'Free at last! Free at last! Thank God Almighty, we are free at last!'"

As she stood on the steps of the Lincoln Memorial listening to King's beautiful words and soaring voice, it was as if Rosa Parks were back in First Baptist Church on that Monday evening when she had first felt the power of his speech.

14 VOTING RIGHTS

We shall overcome.
We shall overcome.
We shall overcome, someday.
For deep in our hearts
we do believe
that we shall overcome
someday.

AFRICAN-AMERICAN FREEDOM SONG

The joy Rosa Parks felt in Washington didn't last long. Only 18 days after the march, on September 15, 1963, violence returned to Birmingham, Alabama. White segregationists in that city threw dynamite into an African-American church there, killing four young girls. On the same day, two black men were killed on the streets of Birmingham. The deaths reminded African Americans that they still had a long and dangerous road ahead of them.

Black people weren't the only victims of these violent times, however. In November 1963, President John F. Kennedy was

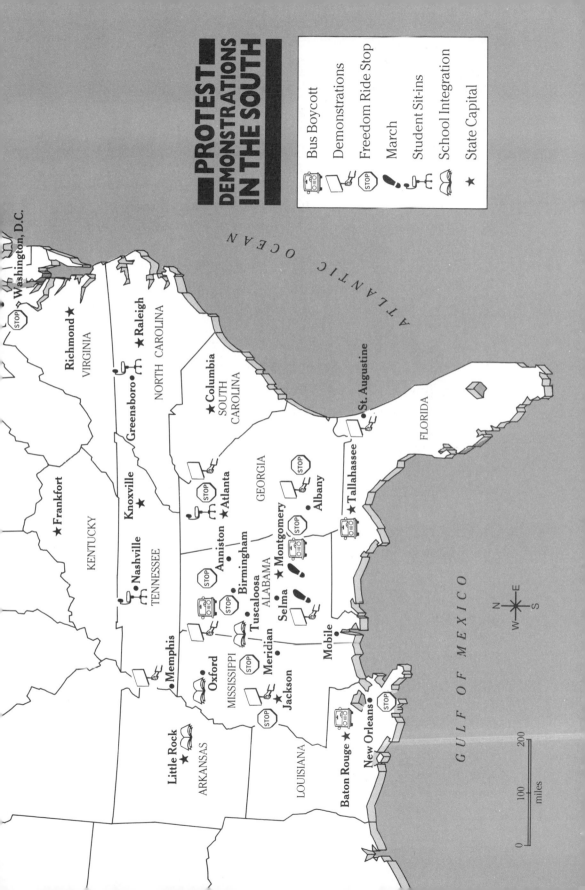

PROTEST DEMONSTRATIONS IN THE SOUTH

Bus Boycott
Demonstrations
Freedom Ride Stop
March
Student Sit-ins
School Integration
★ State Capital

ATLANTIC OCEAN

Washington, D.C.

Richmond ★
VIRGINIA

Greensboro • ★ Raleigh
NORTH CAROLINA

★ Columbia
SOUTH CAROLINA

St. Augustine •

FLORIDA

Frankfort ★
KENTUCKY

Knoxville
★

Nashville •
TENNESSEE

Atlanta
★
GEORGIA

Albany

★ Tallahassee

Memphis •

Oxford •
MISSISSIPPI

Anniston •

Birmingham •
Tuscaloosa •
ALABAMA

Montgomery ★

Selma •

Meridian •
Jackson ★

Mobile •

GULF OF MEXICO

Little Rock ★
ARKANSAS

LOUISIANA

Baton Rouge ★
New Orleans •

N
W — E
S

0   100   200
miles

assassinated by a gunman in Dallas. Seven months later, in June 1964, three CORE workers disappeared in Mississippi. Michael Schwerner and Andrew Goodman, two white men from New York City, and James Earl Chaney, a black Mississippian, had been working to register black voters in the South when they vanished. Two months later, on August 4, their bodies were found buried. They had all been shot. In December, 21 white people from Mississippi—including a policeman—were arrested for the murders.

Still, the work of registering black voters continued. Many brave young workers from the SNCC and the SCLC now went to the town of Selma, in Dallas County, Alabama, where there were 15,000 blacks of voting age but only about 300 registered black voters. The reason was clear enough. Selma's white population didn't want black people to vote. The Dallas County sheriff, Jim Clark, liked to say that blacks couldn't vote because they weren't smart enough. But whenever a black person tried to vote, the police threatened him or her.

Rosa Parks was sad to be so far away from the struggle in Selma. She had done a lot of voter registration work in Montgomery, and she wished she could help now. But her life was now in Detroit, and there was more than enough that needed changing there. During her first years in Detroit, Mrs. Parks had to struggle to support her husband and her mother. Both of them were too ill to work, so she began to work as a seamstress again, just as she had done in Montgomery before the boycott. She joined the St. Matthew's AME Church on Detroit's Delosky Avenue and became a member of the local branch of the NAACP.

There were no segregation laws in Michigan, but in many ways African Americans in Detroit still suffered from racism. The city was run by white men who didn't treat blacks as equals. It was much harder for a black family to find a cheap apartment in the city-owned housing developments than it was for a white family to do so. The city police sometimes arrested or beat up blacks for crimes they didn't commit. Schools in black neighborhoods usually received less money from the city than did the schools in white neighborhoods. Rosa Parks could see that poverty and homelessness were serious problems in the big city. In smaller towns like Montgomery, communities were closer and people helped one another. But in Detroit, when people lost their jobs it wasn't long before they were on the streets. Rosa Parks tried to rebuild some sense of community in her own neighborhood on Detroit's West Side. She organized her friends and neighbors to help her run a small charity. They looked for people who were having difficulty making ends meet, and found clothes and cooked meals for needy families. Still, secondhand clothes and hot meals only helped people to survive. Rosa Parks wanted to see black people getting together to vote, to make city officials listen to their problems. African Americans in Detroit weren't used to making demands. They didn't think they could change anything. But Mrs. Parks could feel that the civil rights movement in the South was beginning to change things—even in Detroit. Many black people in this city had "escaped" from life in the segregated South. Now they could see segregation crumbling just because ordinary people like themselves had gotten together to protest.

In July 1964, the civil rights bill that President Kennedy had sent to Congress finally became an act of law. But the black people of Selma, Alabama, still couldn't vote. When they tried to register, Sheriff Jim Clark and his men often beat or attacked them with cattle prods. In February 1965, the SCLC held a protest march there. The police charged at the protesters. When 26-year-old Jimmie Lee Jackson tried to fight off the policemen who were beating his 82-year-old grandfather and his mother, an officer shot him in the stomach.

The death of Jimmie Lee Jackson made the civil rights leaders demand more new laws to protect black voters. They decided to have a huge five-day-long protest march from Selma to Montgomery, the capital of Alabama.

In March 1965, Rosa Parks flew down from Detroit to join the protest. As she walked along the Jefferson Davis Highway with 25,000 other marchers, she noticed several billboards that had been put up along the way. They carried pictures of Martin Luther King, Jr., at the Highlander School. The captions on the boards read: "Martin Luther King at Communist Training School." Segregationists were still using the fear of communism to attack the civil rights movement.

On Thursday, March 25, the marchers entered Montgomery. Rosa Parks walked beside Martin Luther King, Jr., as they marched through the streets of their old neighborhood. She walked past the doors of the Dexter Avenue Baptist Church, where the MIA held its meetings during the bus boycott. The march ended on the steps of the state capitol building. Many leaders of the civil rights movement spoke to the crowds in Montgomery that day. One of the marchers, a minister from Tennessee, was particularly impressed by a short speech from Rosa Parks. She seemed "fiery" as she talked about the billboards along the highway. Later the minister told his small congregation of Rosa Parks's words:

"My life has been hard. As a small girl I had to run—or thought I had to—from the Ku Klux Klan to escape being killed. My father was cheated out of his land by a white man. I did not get much education. I could not register to vote. I always worked hard for very little. Without education and without being able to vote I tried to be a good citizen. I did attend a workshop at the Highlander School, and I want to tell you that the only reason I don't hate every white man alive is Highlander and Myles Horton."

At the end of the day, Rosa Parks felt only happiness. Nearly 10 years had passed since the days when Montgomery was the "walking city." And here they were again, still walking! Slowly but surely, they were winning the struggle for civil rights.

Five months later, on August 6, 1965, Rosa Parks sat in a room in Washington, D.C., with Martin Luther King, Jr., and other civil rights leaders as President Lyndon B. Johnson signed the Voting Rights Act. This was the new law the marchers had demanded in Selma and Montgomery. It outlawed the literacy tests—including the 24 questions—that election officials in Alabama had used for so many years to keep blacks from the voting booths. They would no longer be able to stop blacks from voting.

All over the South, African Americans began to register to vote. Even in Dallas County, Alabama, Sheriff Jim Clark's home, 9,000 blacks registered within one year after the new act was passed. The sheriff was voted out of his job. Soon African Americans themselves began to run for election.

15 THE MOTHER OF THE MOVEMENT

❝ Sometimes I wonder where we would be if people like Mrs. Parks hadn't been around to help start the Civil Rights Movement. Would we still have segregated buses? Would blacks live a free life or a segregated life? ❞

SHERRI MURPHY, Grade 8, Rosa Parks School, Detroit (cited in the *Michigan Chronicle*, February 22, 1966)

Rosa Parks had something special to thank black voters for in 1965—a new job. For years she worked as a seamstress in Detroit, but she longed for the kind of work she had done in E. D. Nixon's office in the old days. That was a job that allowed her to stay in touch with the problems of ordinary people, as well as with people who could change things. Finally, in the year of the Voting Rights Act, she found what she was looking for in the office of Detroit Congressman John Conyers.

Conyers was a young black member of the U.S. House of Representatives who had recently been elected to his first term. He had just opened an office in the city's Federal Building. He needed someone to run it and to help him stay in touch with the people who had elected him. Rosa Parks was perfect for the job. Soon she was answering phones, typing letters, and following up the problems of people who were having trouble with the city's services. She worked long hours, but she was happy with her new and busy life. Conyers was a popular politician. A newspaper poll listed him as the most important black man in the city. He became a familiar figure in Congress, and Rosa Parks became a familiar figure in the Federal Building.

By the late 1960s, the civil rights movement had achieved many of its original goals. Racial discrimination in the South was beginning to disappear. The many Supreme Court decisions, the Civil Rights Act, and the Voting Rights Act had put an end to the segregation laws of southern states.

While the situation in the South was changing fast, African Americans in the North began to remind the nation that they still faced many injustices. They still had to live with the prejudices and racism of many white people. Unemployment and poverty remained higher among blacks than among whites. They were still all too often the victims of white violence. Many young blacks in northern cities were attracted to groups such as the Black Panthers, which encouraged them to carry guns to defend themselves from white racists. They did not believe in passive resistance and often became involved in gun battles with the police. As a result, many Black Panthers were either killed or imprisoned.

Living in Detroit, Rosa Parks knew just how angry many young African Americans felt. In July 1967, a young black army veteran named Danny Thomas was killed by a gang of white men in Detroit. Two weeks later, the police tried to arrest 100 black men, many of them soldiers on leave from Vietnam, for drinking at an unlicensed bar. The bar, called the Blind Pig, was in the same neighborhood in which Thomas had been murdered. People here were still angry that the police hadn't arrested Danny Thomas's murderers. Yet they were now arresting 100 black men just for drinking illegally. Just as the last of the men was led away from the Blind Pig, an empty bottle smashed into a police car's rear windshield. Someone threw a litter basket threw the window of a store. A young man began yelling, "We're going to have a riot!" and encouraging the crowd to do just that. From her home in the city, Rosa Parks could see the flames of buildings that had been set on fire. The Detroit riots had begun.

John Conyers, Rosa Parks's friend and employer, lived in a part of town that was right in the middle of the rioting. Together with other black community leaders, he drove around the neighborhood asking people to stop rioting and go home. It was no use. Conyers noticed a woman standing in the street with a baby in her arms. She was screaming and cursing "whitey" for no real reason. When he reached Twelfth Street, where some of the worst rioting was taking place, Congressman Conyers climbed on top of the car to speak to the crowds. As he began, he was faced by a man whom he had once defended in court. The man, who was active in the civil rights movement, had been jailed unfairly. Now he was taking out his bitterness by encouraging the rioters. "Why are you defending the cops and the establishment? the man shouted at Conyers. "You're just as bad as they are!"

The rioting went on for seven days. Police officers and soldiers used heavy machine guns to shoot at the rioters. When the rioting stopped, 43 people were dead. Thirty-three of them were black.

The struggles and victories of the civil rights movement hadn't put an end to the anger and violence that so many whites and blacks felt toward one another. One year after the Detroit riots, in April 1968, Martin Luther King, Jr., was murdered by a white gunman in Memphis, Tennessee. Dr. King had gone to Memphis to support a sanitation workers' strike. When he stepped out onto the balcony of his motel room for a breath of air, he was cut down by the bullets of James Earl Ray, who had been waiting for a chance to shoot him. Only two days after Dr. King's death, Bobby Hutton, a Black Panther, was shot to death in Oakland, California. In Chicago, angry blacks began to riot. The city's mayor ordered his policemen to "shoot to kill."

Seeing so much hatred and violence made Rosa Parks wonder sometimes whether it was still possible for whites and blacks to live in peace. "Time is running out for a peaceful solution," she wrote in a letter about racial violence. But she held on to her hope, and she worked in Conyers's office.

In spite of the violence of the late 1960s, blacks did have many reasons to be hopeful about all that had been accomplished during the decade. They had changed forever the way whites looked at them and the way they saw themselves. They had put an end to the laws that supported racial segregation, and they had taken back their right to vote. They had stood up to the threats of the Klansmen. The Ku Klux Klan would never be strong again, and even the WCC was fading away. Gone were the days when white supremacists could terrorize African Americans into quiet obedience. Gone were the days of whites-only water fountains, lunch counters, and waiting rooms. These symbols of the bad old days were replaced by a spirit of hope. Much work remained to be done, but the leaders of the movement could look back on over a decade of unparalleled progress.

The black civil rights protester also inspired many new movements in the 1960s and 1970s. Many white students who had been involved in the workshops of the SNCC and CORE began to set up new organizations on their campuses. At Berkeley, the Free Speech Movement used passive-resistance methods to fight for students' right to campaign on campus. At the University of Michigan in Ann Arbor, Al Haber and Tom Hayden began Students for a Democratic Society (SDS) "as an information and support network for civil rights workers." These new student groups soon became involved in the growing movement to stop the war in Vietnam. South Vietnam was a small Asian country where U.S. troops were fighting against a Communist government called the Viet Cong. Thousands of young Americans had been drafted, or ordered to join the army, to fight in this war. Now some black civil rights groups joined with some student groups to protest against the part the United States was playing in the war. On November 15, 1969, they held a huge antiwar march in Washington, D.C. Then they gathered opposite the Lincoln Memorial, from which Martin Luther King, Jr., had spoken to the civil rights marchers only six years earlier.

The civil rights protests had also been a model for the women's liberation movement, which gained strength during the late 1960s. Feminists wanted women to gain their rights just as blacks had struggled for theirs. One famous feminist, Gloria Steinem, asked in an article in *New York* magazine: "After Black Power, Women's Liberation?" There were many things they wanted to change. For example, women were often prevented from getting good jobs, and they were paid less than men. As they fought to win their rights, many women looked to their "sisters" in the civil rights movement. They admired women like Rosa Parks because they now understood how hard she had fought to win her rights, both as a woman and as an African-American citizen.

Meanwhile, back in Detroit, Rosa Parks had her hands full with her job and the responsibility of looking after her husband and her mother. Both of them were unwell most of the time, and they needed a great deal of care. "I could use a housekeeper," Rosa Parks joked sometimes, but she managed by herself.

Even her co-workers at Conyers's office came to know Rosa Parks as a motherly figure who always brought them food and

After Rosa Parks moved to Detroit, she began working in the office of Senator John Conyers.

told them to "eat right." But they also admired her as a political figure. As one Conyers aide said: "She's on every issue. She's a very nice person, but, man, is she tough. She will take a position and stick to it no matter what."

Rosa Parks's co-workers admired her and all that she had done. It must have been amusing for them to watch the reaction of people who came into the office for the first time and realized whom they were facing at the reception desk. "When they recognize her face," one of them said, "you can tell that some of them almost want to bow down in front of her."

By the middle of the 1970s, Rosa Parks was beginning to be idolized in Detroit. Newspaper editorials called her "our treasure," and the city's Afro-American Museum exhibited a large portrait of her. But she wanted to make good use of her reputation and her influence. She had a special concern for the children growing up in the harsh environment of Detroit's poor neighborhoods. For this reason she made regular appearances at the city's schools to talk to the students and to give them a sense of pride in their people and in themselves.

One school was so taken with Rosa Parks that it changed its name to the Rosa Parks School. The students at that school also wrote letters and essays to express what an inspiration Mrs. Parks was to them. One eighth grader wrote: "What Mrs. Parks means to me: She makes me want to believe in myself. Just because I'm black it doesn't mean I can't get all I want out of my life. She encourages me to stand by what I believe in and not let anyone discourage me."

Rosa Parks also involved herself as much as possible in Detroit's politics. Apart from working for Congressman Conyers, she supported the campaign of Coleman Alex Young for mayor. He became the city's first black mayor in 1973. As she said later, "The time for a black mayor was well past due." She also became involved in the movement to end apartheid in South Africa. In South Africa, black people live with a system of racial segregation laws (called apartheid) that are even stricter than those in the South of this country had been. Unlike the United States, though, the white population of South Africa is a small minority. The South African constitution supports apartheid. In many ways, apartheid echoes the years of segregation in the United States in strange ways. The South African government has tried to defend its apartheid policies with the motto of "separate but equal." Rosa Parks had heard that one before. Those were the words the U.S. Supreme Court had used when it made segregation legal in the *Plessy* v. *Ferguson* case of 1896.

The legal system in the United States had been slow to change and to give justice to African Americans. But it had changed for the better. In 1976, Rosa and Raymond Parks saw encouraging proof of this. That October, Clarence Norris, the last surviving "Scottsboro boy," received his pardon from Alabama's Governor George Wallace. Norris was now an old man. He lived in the Bronx, New York, and had not been to Alabama for many years. But the pardon meant a great deal to him and to those who had worked in the Scottsboro campaign, such as Raymond Parks. According to Alabama law, a pardon could be given only "on grounds of innocence." Although it had come 40 years too late, it was good to hear that the Alabama governor believed Norris was innocent.

In spite of the good news about Clarence Norris, 1976 wasn't a happy year for Rosa Parks. It was the year in which her mother died. The very next year, Raymond Parks passed away. Then, in 1978, her brother Sylvester became ill and died. Within just three years, Rosa Parks had lost all of her closest relatives.

It was a very sad time, and Rosa Parks had to keep busy in order to survive it. She often went out of town on speaking engagements, or to one of the many functions at which awards have been presented to her. In 1979, she won the NAACP's highest honor, the Spingarn Medal. This award had been given to many great African Americans over the years. Martin Luther King, Jr., had won it, and so had NAACP president Roy Wilkins and the famous musician Duke Ellington. It was quite an honor. In 1980, Rosa Parks traveled to Atlanta, Georgia, to receive the Martin Luther King, Jr., Nonviolent Peace Prize from the hands of Coretta Scott King. Four years later, she received the Wonder Woman Foundation's Special 1984 Eleanor Roosevelt Woman of Courage Award.

By this time, Rosa Parks was turning into a celebrity. In May 1984, Gloria Steinem held a grand party at New York City's Waldorf Astoria Hotel. The party was held to raise money for the Ms. Foundation, a charity run by the magazine for which Steinem worked. Many famous people were there, including Sally Ride, the United States's first woman in space; Bella Abzug, the former U.S. congresswoman from New York City; and Phil Donahue, the TV talk-show host. Among them, as a star guest, was Rosa Parks. She was even mentioned in the society column of the New York *Daily News* the next day by a writer who praised "the dignity and beauty of Rosa Parks."

This was all very flattering, but Rosa Parks was getting used

Rosa Parks Honored

In 1955, Rosa Parks refused to give up her right to sit down on a public bus seat. Her action led to a bus boycott and sparked an entire movement. Parks is called the mother of the civil rights movement. Since then she has become a symbol for overcoming oppression, prejudice, and injustice.

Rosa Parks showed how one individual can resist an unfair law and change the face of a nation.

President Jimmy Car-
ter, First Lady
Rosalynn Carter, and
Rosa Parks at the
1978 Congressional
Black Caucus dinner.

Rosa Parks is
awarded the Medal
of Freedom, the high-
est honor given to a
citizen of the United
States.

119

to her second career as a public figure. The year 1985 was particularly busy. She made many appearances for a variety of occasions, such as the 30th anniversary of the bus boycott, the first Martin Luther King, Jr. holiday, and the annual activities for Black History Month in Detroit.

In August of the same year, Rosa Parks spoke at a large antiapartheid rally in Detroit. Two thousand protesters cheered as she approached the microphone. The chanting crowd was dotted with children, and Mrs. Parks was reminded of the freedom songs she had learned from her mother when she was a child. "Someone recently asked me when children should learn about the struggle," she said over the microphones. "I told them, as soon as they're born. You can't begin too soon. Things will get better when we make them better by getting together in love, unity, and goodwill."

In 1986, Rosa Parks ran for election to the NAACP board and supported a slate of other candidates as well. One newspaper article at the time tried to suggest that someone like her shouldn't take part in the NAACP elections. The article called her "our nation's treasure" but said it would be a mistake "in the golden years of her life to get caught up in the vicious in-fights" of the NAACP. Rosa Parks was quick to respond with an article of her own saying she wanted to be a part of NAACP politics. "I made my own choice in supporting the slate that I did and have not felt as though I was being 'exploited,'" she wrote. She won the election easily, along with her slate of candidates.

Rosa Parks knew that people liked to look up to her, but she didn't want to be hidden away just because she had been called a treasure. In 1987, she began the Rosa and Raymond Parks Institute for Self-Development. That same year, she won the Roger Joseph Prize, an honor that came with a cash award of $10,000. She used the money to help fund the institute. The purpose of the Institute for Self-Development was to encourage young people to work for change and to fulfill their own potential. The institute tried to teach young people about the struggles of the civil rights movement as well. It helped to organize a bus tour that took an interracial group of 37 youths along the route of the Freedom Rides of the 1960s. Rosa Parks accompanied the group.

As they traveled through the South, the group visited the bus stops and waiting rooms of Birmingham and Montgomery, where the Freedom Riders had been beaten and arrested. They rode along the highway in Anniston, where the Freedom Riders' bus had been firebombed in 1961. Now, in the 1980s, blacks and whites could travel together anywhere in the United States without fear. The young passengers in the bus with Rosa Parks were learning an important lesson—that many of the freedoms they now took for granted had been won not so long ago by ordinary but brave people who decided to speak out for what they believed was right.

Rosa Parks has never stopped speaking out for her beliefs. She always wanted to take part and to take sides. That was why she didn't quietly give up her bus seat in 1955. She took part in the NAACP elections for the same reason. Rosa Parks played a part in yet another election in 1988, when she supported Jesse Jackson's campaign for the presidency. By joining Jackson at the Democratic National Convention in Atlanta, she made sure that everyone understood whose side she was on.

Standing next to Jesse Jackson in the Atlanta hotel meeting room as he comforted his delegates, Rosa Parks knew that he understood the importance of taking part. He had run for president even when all the newspapers told him that it was hopeless for a black man to do so. By running, Jackson had changed things a little. The next time, it would be that much easier for an African American to run—and to win. "Today's protests are tomorrow's mainstream," Jackson told the delegates, and Rosa Parks began to smile. She was already looking forward to the next elections.

Timetable of Events
in the Life of
Rosa Parks

Feb. 4, 1913	Born in Pine Level, Alabama
1926	Attends Booker T. Washington Junior High School
1928	Attends Alabama State College
1932	Marries Raymond Parks
1934	Receives high-school diploma
1943	Joins National Association for the Advancement of Colored People (NAACP)
1954	Organizes NAACP youth group in Montgomery, Alabama
1955	Attends workshop at Highlander Folk School
1955	Is arrested for breaking bus segregation laws
1957	Moves to Detroit, Michigan
1962	Attends Southern Christian Leadership Conference (SCLC) convention in Birmingham, Alabama
1963	Is honored at March on Washington
1965	Participates in Selma to Montgomery march
1965	Begins working in Michigan Congressman John Conyers's office
1979	Awarded the Spingarn Medal
1986	Is elected to the board of the Detroit branch of the NAACP
1988	Is featured at the Democratic National Convention with Jesse Jackson

SUGGESTED READING

Afro-American Encyclopedia. Miami, Florida: Educational Book Publishers, 1974.

Branch, Taylor. *Parting the Waters: America in the King Years 1954–63*. New York: Simon and Schuster, 1988.

Brown, Cynthia and Septima Clarke. *Ready from Within*. Navarro: Wild Trees Press, 1986.

Giddings, Paula. *When and Where I Enter: The Impact of Black Women on Race and Sex in America*. New York: William Morrow, 1984.

*Greenfield, Eloise. *Rosa Parks*. New York: Crowell, 1973.

*Meriwether, Louise. *Don't Ride the Bus on Monday—The Rosa Parks Story*. Englewood Cliffs: Prentice Hall, 1973.

Metcalf, George. *Black Profiles*. New York: McGraw-Hill, 1968.

Morris, Aldon. *The Origins of the Civil Rights Movement*. New York: The Free Press, 1984.

Raines, Howell. *My Soul is Rested: Movement Days in the Deep South Remembered*. New York: Bantam, 1978.

Williams, Juan. *Eyes on the Prize: America's Civil Rights Years 1954–1965*. New York: Viking Penguin, 1987.

---

*Readers of *Rosa Parks: The Movement Organizes* will find these books particularly readable.

SOURCES

Afro-American Encyclopedia. Miami, Florida: Educational Book Publishers, 1974.

Branch, Taylor. *Parting the Waters: America in the King Years 1954–63*. New York: Simon and Schuster, 1988.

Brown, Cynthia, and Septima Clarke. *Ready from Within*. Navarro: Wild Trees Press, 1986.

Giddings, Paula. *When and Where I Enter: The Impact of Black Women on Race and Sex in America*. New York: William Morrow, 1984.

Grant, Joanne. *Black Protest, History Documents and Analyses 1619 to the Present*. New York: Fawcett, 1968.

Greenfield, Eloise. *Rosa Parks*. New York: Crowell, 1973.

Meriwether, Louise. *Don't Ride the Bus on Monday—The Rosa Parks Story*. Englewood Cliffs: Prentice Hall, 1973.

Metcalf, George. *Black Profiles*. New York: McGraw-Hill, 1968.

Morris, Aldon. *The Origins of the Civil Rights Movement*. New York: The Free Press, 1984.

Raines, Howell. *My Soul is Rested: Movement Days in the Deep South Remembered*. New York: Bantam, 1978.

Williams, Juan. *Eyes on the Prize: America's Civil Rights Years 1954–1965*. New York: Viking Penguin, 1987.

RESEARCH LIBRARY

Metcalf, George R. Papers. The Schomburg Center for Research in Black Culture, The New York Public Library, New York.

INDEX

Abernathy, Ralph, 57, 58, 72, 78, 83, 88
Abzug, Bella, 117
Afro-American Museum, 115
Alabama State College, 25, 28
Alabama Supreme Court, 30
Apartheid, 116

Baker, Ella, 35, 95, 97
Bates, Ruby, 30
The Birth of a Nation (film), 14
Black Panthers, 111, 113
Blake, James F., 32, 53
Booker T. Washington Junior High, Montgomery, 24–25
Boycott
  of Montgomery buses, 56–85
  of Montgomery streetcars, 20–21
  of Washington streetcars, 21–22
Briggs case, 38
Brotherhood of Sleeping Car Porters, 34, 36
Brown v. *Board of Education* case, 38, 43
Buses
  boycott, 56–85
  segregation, 31–33
  violence over integration, 86–91

Central High School, Little Rock, integrated, 94–95
Chaney, James Earl, 106
Children's protest march, 101–103
Churches bombed, 88–89
Civil Rights Act (1957), 103
Civil Rights Act (1964), 103, 111
Civil War, 12–14, 21
Clark, Jim, 106, 109
Clark, Septima, 50–51, 95, 96
Colvin, Claudette, 40, 55, 62
Congress of Racial Equality (CORE), 98, 113
Constitution, 23–25, 41
  Fifteenth Amendment, 14
Conyers, John, 111–113

The Crisis, 34
Crusade for Citizenship, 95, 97

Davis, Jefferson, 19
Declaration of Independence, 41
Desegregation of armed forces, 35
Dexter Avenue Baptist Church, Montgomery, 19–20, 38–39, 64, 108
Diggs, Charles C., 91
Donahue, Phil, 117
Dukakis, Michael, 5
Durr, Clifford, 35, 40, 46–47, 55
Durr, Virginia, 35, 46–48

Edwards, Rose, 25
Edwards, Sylvester, 8, 11, 25
Eisenhower, Dwight D., 97
Ellington, Duke, 117

Fifteenth Amendment, 14
First Baptist Church, Montgomery, 57–58, 64
Ford Motor Company, 91
Freedom Riders, 98–100
Freedom Train, 41, 51
Free Speech Movement, 113–114
Fugitive Slave Law, 12

Gandhi, Mohandas (Mahatma), 75
Goodman, Andrew, 106
Graetz, Robert, 39, 88
Grandfather clause, 33
Gray, Fred, 40, 55, 56, 62, 74
Great Depression, 28

Haber, Al, 114
Hayden, Tom, 114
Highlander Folk School, 47–51, 79, 94, 96–97, 108
Horton, Myles, 47, 48–50
Hutton, Bobby, 113

"I Have a Dream" speech (King), 103

Jackson, Jesse, 5–7, 121
Jackson, Jimmy Lee, 107
Jim Crow laws, 20
Johns, Barbara, 38–39
Johnson, Lyndon B., 109
Johns, Vernon, 39
Jones, Curtis, 43

Kennedy, John F., 97, 103, 104–106
King, Coretta Scott, 82–83, 117
King, Martin Luther, Jr., 38–39,
    57–85, 90–91, 101, 108, 113, 117
Ku Klux Klan, 8–11, 14–15, 29, 39,
    113

Lee, George, 43
Lincoln, Abraham, 13
Little Rock Nine, 94, 97
Lynchings, 9, 14, 33, 43–44

McCauley, James, 15
McCauley, Leona, 9, 15, 16–17, 28,
    55, 90, 117
McCauley, Rosa. See Parks, Rosa
    McCauley
McCauley, Sylvester, 9, 15, 91, 92,
    117
March on Washington, 103, 114
Martin Luther King, Jr.,
    Nonviolent Peace Prize, 117
Maxwell Air Force Base, 28, 35
Meredith, James, 100
Michigan, University of, 114
Miscegenation, 15, 26
Mississippi, University of, 100
Montgomery Fair Department
    Store, 52, 79
Montgomery Improvement
    Association (MIA), 64, 69,
    72–73, 81–82, 84
Montgomery Industrial School for
    Girls, 18–19
Montgomery Voters' League, 35
Mrs. White's School for Girls,
    18–19
Ms.Foundation, 117

National Association for the
    Advancement of Colored
    People (NAACP), 33–34, 36,
    78–79, 94–95

New York Daily News, 117
New York magazine,114
New York State Emancipation Act
    (1827), 21
Nixon, E. D., 34, 36, 37, 40,
    55–56, 62, 64–68, 72, 76, 83,
    90–91
Nixon, Richard M., 97
Norris, Clarence, 116–117

Parks, Geri, 26
Parks, Raymond, 25–27, 30, 33, 35,
    45–47, 55, 79–80, 88, 90, 117
Parks, Rosa McCauley
    arrested, 54–55
    and bus boycott, 56–85
    completes education, 27–28
    in Detroit, 91–93
    at Highlander Folk School, 47–51
    honors, 116–120
    loses department store job, 79
    marries, 27
    on NAACP board, 120–121
    at SCLC convention, 100–101
    at Selma-to-Montgomery protest
        march, 108
    at signing of Voting Rights Act,
        109
    and violence over integration of
        buses, 88–90
    works for John Conyers, 111, 113
    works for NAACP, 34–37
Passive resistance, 75
Pleasant, Mary Ellen, 22
Plessy v. Ferguson, 23
Poll tax, 35

Randolph, A. Phillip, 34
Ray, James Earl, 113
Ride, Sally, 117
Riots, 112–113
Robinson, Jo Ann, 35, 40, 57
Roger Joseph Prize, 120
Rosa and Raymond Parks Institute
    for Self-Development, 120–121
Rosa Parks School, 116

Saint Paul Methodist Church, 59
San Francisco Trolley Co., 22
Schwerner, Michael, 106
Scottsboro boys, 29–30, 116–117

Segregation, 22–25, 35, 82–85
"Separate but equal" facilities,
    23–24
Sharecropping, 13
Shaw University, 97
Sit-ins, 95–96
Slave rebellion, 11–12
Southern Christian Leadership
    Conference (SCLC), 90, 93, 95,
    100–101
Spingarn Medal, 117
Steinem, Gloria, 114, 117
Student Nonviolent Coordinating
    Committee (SNCC), 97, 113
Students for a Democratic Society
    (SDS), 114
Supreme Court, 23, 33, 38, 82

Thomas, Danny, 111–112
Till, Emmett, 43–44
Trinity Lutheran Church,
    Montgomery, 39, 58, 59
Truman, Harry S., 35
Truth, Sojourner, 21–22
Tubman, Harriet, 12–13, 41
Turner, Nat, 11–12
Tuskegee Institute, 15

Underground Railroad, 12, 41

Vietcong, 114
Vietnam War, 114
Violence over bus integration, 86–91
Voter registration, 95, 97
Voting rights, 14, 33
Voting Rights Act (1965), 109, 111

Waldorf Astoria Hotel, 117
Wallace, George, 116
Washington, Booker T., 15
Washington, March on, 103, 114
White Citizens' Council (WCC), 43,
    72, 94, 113
Wilkins, Roy, 34, 117
Women's Political Council (WPC),
    35, 56–57
Wonder Woman Foundation's
    Special 1984 Eleanor Roosevelt
    Woman of Courage Award, 117
World War I, 15
World War II, 32

Young, Coleman Alex, 116

About the Author

Kai Jabir Friese has an M.A. degree in political science from the University of Pennsylvania. Born in Hyderabad, India, Friese has lived in Western Europe and America for most of the last decade. He is the author of a biography, *Tenzin Gyatso, the Dalai Lama of Tibet.*